What They're Sayin
Let Your Music Soar

Let Your Music Soar returns music to those who love and make it. Corky Siegel's book—so beautifully accompanied by Holly's pointed and amusing artwork—offers immensely practical insights into how to draw out the music that is within us and share it with others.

Reading this book will make you want to pick up the ukulele or blues harp you haven't played since the seventh grade, or help you unlock the true note of personality that even accomplished professional players can neglect. It is peppered with sentences that make you slap your forehead and say, "Of course! It's so clear now. Gotta try that!" Thirty years of trial, error, and joy have been distilled into a bracing and entertaining brew.

—**Scott Simon**, Peabody Award Winner, National Public Radio Host of W*eekend Edition*

This book is a perfect way to begin to free yourself to become confident enough to allow your own creativity to flow. Corky provides a starting point and through a series of logical, user-friendly techniques, puts you on the path where you can spend the rest of your life making music of your own. The book reflects his artistry and originality as an outstanding soloist, composer and improviser, and reading this book is as much fun as playing music with him. Highly recommended for all ages!

—**David Amram**, Former Composer-in-Residence at the New York Philharmonic, Conductor, Multi-Instrumentalist, Author

I am walking around rather amazed today. I spent some time practicing this morning, playing Bach and exploring your ideas and suggestions. What has occurred defies description. The way I play seems to have fundamentally changed and improved overnight. I can't actually believe it, but I think it is true.

—**Michael Miles**, Music Education Director, Old Town School of Folk Music

In your master classes for our grade and high schools, you took our students to the next level, thanks to your years of observing and educating. The directors say you changed their perspectives on dynamics too. Your book reminds us that music should be fun—the drawings make us chuckle and realize that even high level performers can retain a sense of humor about this "serious stuff."

—**Chris Bank**, Director of In-School Programs, Jazz Aspen Snowmass

Corky's own life's encounters support this endearing presentation, creating a learning experience that captivates its readers. Masterful, insightful, filled with light and passion, he reaches into the deepest depths of his soul and offers a resourceful learning experience. A must for any music aficionado.

—**Salli Squitieri** and **Gabriel Butterfield,** The Paul Butterfield Fund and Society

What a fantastic work! It should be required reading for any musician, whether you're an amateur or a seasoned pro.

—**Ellis Kell**, Music Columnist, *The Rock Island Argus, The Dispatch* and *The Leader*

The Thor Story should be spread around like the Bible.

—**Patrick McAllister**, Entrepreneur and Singer/Songwriter

When Corky Siegel worked with our sixth-, seventh-, and eighth-grade bands, he picked me, the Mean Ol' Music Teacher, to demonstrate "forceful" and "delicate" dynamic playing. My seventh-graders just loved it! Corky literally changed my playing within minutes.

The simple concept of using dynamics and articulation to vary the music truly transforms MUSIC from two to three dimensions and makes the emotional connection unmistakable. Thus a new term has evolved with my classes. We call it "Corkifying," as in, "Come on, let's Corkify that section!" The kids know what it means and always respond. My classes are excited about MUSIC!

—**Mark Gray**, Performer, Music Educator, Roaring Fork High School and Carbondale Middle School, Carbondale, Colorado

Hallelujah! I have just read, learned, been inspired, cracked-up, and soared through my first of many readings of this book. Holly's illustrations are super-cool! After years of writing and coaching vocal improv, I'm re-invigorated. I can express things better with my students and in workshops and am more "Sue," with no apologies, in my own performances.

—**Sue Demel**, Educator and Singer, *Sons of the Never Wrong*

LET YOUR MUSIC SOAR

LET YOUR MUSIC SOAR

The Emotional Connection

Revised Edition

CORKY SIEGEL & PETER KRAMMER

Illustrations by Holly Siegel

Let Your Music Soar: The Emotional Connection

Corky Siegel and Peter Krammer
Illustrations by Holly Siegel
Book design by Annette Krammer

Revised Edition

Websites
For more information, writing, examples, and updates, visit the
Let Your Music Soar website at www.chamberblues.com/soar

Visit www.chamberblues.com to find out more about Corky Siegel or
write him at soar@chamberblues.com.

*Special thanks to Jim Tullio and Ken Goerres for their technical work on
the audio CD and to Jerry Robin and Bob Lange for their input.*

ISBN 978-90-77256-26-8
D/2007/9797/2
Printed in Singapore
20 19 18 17 16 15 14 13 12 11 10 9 8 7 6 5 4 3 2

Table of Contents

Welcome!

For 30 years, Corky Siegel has been sharing with musicians all over the world—professionals as well as beginners—how to tap the natural dynamic power in their music, with amazing results. Experienced in coaching individual players and singers as well as choral groups, symphonies, rock, jazz, folk, and classical ensembles, Corky offers us a rare opportunity to take our performance swiftly to new levels— and let our music soar!

 ## Who Is This Book For?

This book is especially for musicians who want to reach their musical goals quickly and effectively. It is also for anyone interested in the world of artistic expression.

What Is This Book About?

This book has five parts:

- **Healthy Perspective**
  Part One offers a healthy perspective for the performing artist.
  It dispels the fears and misconceptions that suppress artistic expression.

- **Understanding the Benefits of Dynamics**
  Part Two digs deeply into the science of dynamic variation. Understanding how it works and knowing its benefits and expressive power will help assure it won't be forgotten.

- **Applying the Power of Dynamic Expression**
  Part Three introduces The Incredible One-Minute Exercise. It will pull you deeper into your own expression, and automatically fill your performance with color, dimension, fun, excitement, and passion.

- **FAQs and Additional Suggestions**
  Part Four answers questions that lots of musicians have. You'll also find a page of a musical score. It represents part of the complete violin solo performed on the accompanying CD. Even if you don't read music, you can analyze the dynamic symbols as you listen to the piece.

- **Audio Examples Companion CD**
  The CD that comes with this book will help you hear what we are talking about. Set it up so you can read, pause and listen, then read further.

Preface

Sometime in early 1995, I enrolled in a class Corky Siegel was teaching at Columbia College in Chicago. The class, mentioned in a promotional article about Corky in the Sunday news magazine, claimed that in three or four days, Corky would show you how to bring out the emotional elements of your music and put you in control of your performance. In the article, Corky looked so unassuming, lying on his side in a designer sweater, propped up by his elbow, holding up his harmonica, smiling through that ever-present beard of his. Little did I know that by enrolling in the class, not only would my music change, but my life would change as well.

My experiences with Corky started in 1972, at the start of my musical journey. I spent hundreds of hours listening to Corky's solo and Siegel-Schwall Band records as I learned to play the harmonica. These records, along with a few others, stood out like gems in my collection. Over the years, I bought every Corky record that came out and went to every one of his concerts that I could. Although my musical journey has taken many turns, as everybody's journey does, Corky has remained a significant and continuing influence on my music.

Corky's musical journey, as those who are familiar with him know, has been a very interesting one. Emerging from the 1960s Chicago blues scene with people like Buddy Guy, Junior Wells and Paul Butterfield, Corky and his partners in the Siegel-Schwall Band played music that was totally uplifting and highly personal. The songs about insanity didn't make you feel too bad and the party tunes made you feel like you were part of the happening. Over the past 40 years, Corky has continued to write and perform incredible heartfelt gems with his awesome harmonica and piano playing, usually with some other great musicians backing him up.

What I find really interesting is Corky's concurrent career as a globetrotting symphony soloist and his collaborations with Seiji Ozawa and the late Bill Russo. His immersion into the classical form has given rise to one of the truly fine musical inventions of the twentieth century, Chamber Blues. For over 20 years, Corky has continued to compose and perform music that juxtaposes all of the musical elements in the "Corky-universe." He has an extensive body of "opuses," as he calls them, and they are performed by his amazing Chamber Blues ensemble, a group of dedicated, virtuoso musicians that brings Corky's musical jewels to life.

The foundation of Corky's music is love, truth, and an incredible emotional connection—between Corky and his instruments, between the music and the musicians, between the musicians and the listeners. Is it just the virtuosity of the musicians or Corky's compositional prowess on display? These elements are certainly part of the experience, but I don't think that by themselves they cause the experience to happen.

Walking into that Columbia College classroom, I came face-to-face with not only one of our great musical messengers, but with a great musical message. Corky's message contains "the secret," the one piece of the puzzle within reach of every musician, professional or amateur, soloist or ensemble player. When Corky asked me to help with this book, I jumped in with both feet. I have seen these techniques work personally, and by watching Corky coach other musicians, I have come to understand how these techniques are a large part of what makes so many of the great musicians sound so great.

Please accept this offering and watch (and listen to) how its musical message will make your music soar.

Peter Krammer

Introduction
Exploring the Horizons of Musical Expression

🎵 The Secret is Out

I am a mad lover of the art of music. I am a lover of those who love music. I am a lover of those at any skill level who play music. I have stumbled upon an approach to musical coaching that quickly transforms the musical experience and performance of singers and musicians, choruses, bands, orchestras and ensembles. This approach fosters a profound and immediate improvement in the richness of individual and group tonal quality, balance, and listening skills. This approach also intensifies the music, making it more interesting, more musical, more exciting, and more passionate for both the performer and the listener. The performer accomplishes his or her artistic intent with much more ease. Dry old songs come to life. The performer gets in touch with a fresh spontaneity and discovers a new level of confidence whereby playing music, any kind of music, becomes fun again.

I have been sharing this approach to musical performance for over 30 years. Throughout this period, I have continued to dig very deeply into the nature and practicality of this approach, exploring and experimenting every step of the way.

Now it is time to make it available, in depth, to anyone who wants it. As such a lover of music, how can I possibly keep this secret to myself?

I am walking around rather amazed today. I spent some time practicing this morning, playing Bach and exploring your ideas and suggestions. What has occurred defies description. I know you've seen the impact this has on people—you can add me to the list. The way I play seems to have fundamentally changed and improved overnight. I can't actually believe it, but I think it is true.

—Michael Miles, Music Education Director, Old Town School of Folk Music

I know that using this approach will help deepen your experience of music whether you are a beginner or an expert. Consider this secret yours—for you and for your students.

🎵 The Method

The secret method of my approach to musical performance is based on the application of a constant flow (both subtle and extreme) of intensity variation. Intensity variation is the variation of physical intensity and does not rely on sound. Intensity variation involves motion, tension, release, and pressure. Because of this effort, a variation in sound level occurs, between loud and soft. We call this "dynamic variation." The technique we will explore in this book focuses on intensity variation. The result will be dynamic variation.

Though understanding how and why this works is invaluable in guiding one into fuller emotional expression, the technique itself is extremely simple and easy to grasp. In a very short time, you can execute the technique and experience its power and value. This is true for all musicians: young children, new-to-music musicians, experienced amateurs and professionals, and even "masters."

Easy to Grasp

I once coaxed a junior high-aged singer up on stage with an audience of her peers listening in. She was very, very shy. Her shoulders were hunched and she was bent forward with her head down. She did not seem happy about this. After about five minutes of coaching, she began to sing more delicately and more forcefully. Her singing jumped to life! The school principal told me she felt goose bumps. After a short while, the singer turned and faced the audience as a new confidence poured out of her. Her posture improved and at the end, she walked off the stage wearing a big smile as the audience cheered. To me, she seemed like a different person, just from learning about being delicate, strong, and forceful. Her teacher was amazed as she whispered to me, "I didn't know she could sing like that. I didn't know she could produce such a tone—and it happened in front of my eyes. You never even mentioned tone!"

I remember a ten-year-old student who had been studying piano for just a short time. After a brief coaching session, she said, "Oh, you mean you vary the intensity like the waves on the ocean?" Yes. And then she proceeded to play the music with surprising emotion, as if she had been playing for years. Her hands and body relaxed, and she moved spontaneously with the music.

So, if it is so easy, why don't we hear it and do it more?

Difficult to Hold

There is a thick cloud of psychology, and a lot of mythology, around musical performance. All of this "stuff" adds so many distractions and confusions, that it often feels easier to simply ignore something like dynamics than to give it the kind of attention it needs. Of course, this leads to habitually thinking on only one dynamic level. I call this tendency "flat-lining." The music wants to dance but we put the squeeze on it. Even musicians who know the importance of dynamic variation, who use it often in performance, have "moments of weakness." These can occur when performing for what they might think is a challenging audience, feeling too much excitement, trying to play especially well in a recording studio, playing in a dry room, or performing music that seems uninteresting at the time. All of this makes it difficult to hang on consistently to dynamics, that jewel that is so easy to grasp, yet so hard to hold.

I offered a master class to a friend of mine who is a professional musician. He mastered the technique quickly and did, in fact, realize its importance. After our lesson, he stayed to listen in on a class I gave to three other musicians. My friend told me he would never play music with "the old approach" again. A few days later he visited for dinner and I asked him to play for our other guests. He played beautifully, but hardly applied any dynamics! The next day he told me he realized right after the performance that he had forgotten to apply dynamic variation. He was disappointed because he knew how much more exciting and beautiful his performance would have been if he had applied a dynamic flow. Even though the dynamic variation technique is simple to apply, it is darn hard for most people to hang on to it!

With all of the challenges we face in music performance, the dynamic possibilities, which are of astonishing importance, usually take a back seat, if they even get to ride in the bus at all. Although dynamics offers a storehouse of excitement, musicality, and deeper possibilities of expression, the elements of pitch and rhythm demand accuracy and, therefore, seem to require our constant and undivided attention. The dynamic element doesn't crave accuracy; it only craves spontaneity and intensity. Therefore, our reasonable and natural tendency is to put all of our attention into the pitch, rhythm, and melody. This tendency reinforces the need to put "getting it right" ahead of "getting it good." Is the ultimate goal of music performance accuracy or expression?

The good news is that a focus on dynamics supports technical, creative and emotional considerations. Understanding how this works will give you a little more security when diving wholeheartedly into dynamic variation.

♪ This Book's Intent

My intent is to offer a method, along with reliable and practical tools, which will simply make your music soar. Along with that, I offer you information to assure you that using this book and using dynamic variation will help you have more faith in your own inspiration and creativity.

Individual self-expression in music is a pure offering. This perspective takes ideas like "good music" and "bad music" and the "should" and "shouldn't" and reveals them for what they are: unnecessary distractions. This perspective also emphasizes the beauty and value of music and self-expression, something we all know makes this world a better place. I believe this perspective also makes it easier to play and experience music to its fullest.

My wish is that every time you approach your music, whether alone, in practice, in front of a few friends, or on the stage, that your experience is a fun, exciting, passionate and uplifting one.

Part One
Putting Things in Perspective

There is a beautiful little white schoolhouse on top of a hill overlooking the ocean in the Virgin Islands. A couple years ago, I gave a lecture and demonstration to some high school and grade school students. All the windows in the school were open and we could feel the cooling breeze and hear the birds singing and the sounds of occasional cars driving by. It was very sweet. I was describing music to these students from a particular perspective. At that moment, we all heard the distant tone of a horn sounding on a barge far below on the ocean. It was a sound that added to the sweetness of the environment and gave everybody this cozy feeling, reminding us all that we were in this wonderful, exotic place.

I asked the students how this sound made them feel. They confirmed my sentiments. I asked them how the sound of the horn would feel if they were on the ocean and the barge was coming at them. "I would feel very scared," one replied. Other students explained that they would feel anger coming from the barge. The horn would be saying, "Get out of the way!" I told the students that there were two perspectives to consider here. One was down below on the ocean with the barge coming at them and the other was way up on the hill in this beautiful schoolhouse. From down below, the horn feels angry. From up above, it simply adds to the beauty we are experiencing in our life. I explained to them we would talk about music from the high perspective, where you can not only see the whole picture and how everything fits, with all the relationships working, but also how to interpret information from a very beautiful and pure place.

Although there are many "perspectives" to choose from in music, I choose to experience music from "up on the hill" rather than "down on the ocean." I have found the "up on the hill" perspective to be a huge benefit to my own freedom of self-expression.

To share this perspective, and to clean the slate of preconceptions, I always begin by telling the story of Thor.

THOR'S STORY—HOW MUSIC WAS BORN

 Once upon a time, a long, long time ago, before the time of recorded history, even before prerecorded history, and long before the birth of music, before anyone knew anything about music, there lived a cave man named Thor. Thor is the hero of our story. One day Thor was walking around in the forest with nothing to do. He stumbled upon a cave and there he came upon something he had never seen nor could have imagined.

There in the dark shadow and deep silence of the cave stood an amazing sight, an awesome... giant... nine-foot... Steinway grand piano. To make a long story short, after he warmed up to the idea, Thor finally sat down at the bench and pushed a key.

Out of the stillness and silence of the cave popped a beautiful tone. It floated along, shimmered and sparkled for a while, and then slowly faded back into the silence and stillness of the cave. It was a beautiful and amazing experience for Thor. He was enraptured. He did it again. What a sweet, wonderful, gorgeous, lush, sound!

Sound and Silence

Sometimes as musicians we forget how beautiful one sound on an instrument can be. It fills the room and permeates every cell in the body with an uplifting quality.

Just one note on an instrument illustrates the beauty of sound. If we could remember how beautiful one tone on an instrument can be, how could we musicians ever go wrong? Sound is very powerful, but music is not only sound. It is both sound and silence. In fact, silence empowers sound and sound empowers silence.

Out of this play of sound and silence come the beautiful elements of music that include pitch, rhythm, harmony, melody, articulation, dynamic variation, and counterpoint.

Exercise

The power of silence can be illustrated with this exercise. Say the following statement aloud, without any pause between the words:

"The essence of music is the relationship between sound and silence."

How does that sound? How does that feel?

Now, repeat the statement, but with some pauses:

"The essence of music.........is the relationship......between sound............and silence."

Does it seem as if the silence or pauses between the words have almost as much power as the words themselves? Is there potential for another level of emotional experience with the addition of silence between some words? Does it seem as if the meaning of the words hits the target more effectively when silence is used? It is the same way in music. Your music can make its point more effectively when you use silence. The music will more readily hit its target when you allow silence to play its role.

The Experience of Sound and Silence

There is a subtler way of experiencing the power of silence in music. Find a very quiet spot and notice the power and intensity of silence. If you notice a quiet sound in the distance you can still feel the intensity of the silence. If you hear a louder sound, the power of silence is less intense. But in both cases you can feel both the power of sound and the power of silence in different qualities. This is the play of sound and silence. This is also how we experience the feel of sound and silence.

When I talk about sound, I generally refer to the cliché that a tree falling in the forest does not make a sound if no one is there to hear it. This is a very practical perspective. The string on the cello is plucked, but this is not sound—it is just a string vibrating back and forth. No sound has hit the ear yet. Once the string is plucked, air molecules around it begin to vibrate. These molecules in turn hit other molecules and eventually this vibration of air molecules hits our eardrums and makes them vibrate. Even this is not sound. It is just molecules pushing on a piece of flesh that is now just moving back and forth.

This vibration moves through the inner ear and is eventually turned into electrical energy in the cochlea. This electrical energy is not sound—it is just pulsating electrical energy. None of these events is sound. They are only stimuli that create an experience of sound. According to this perspective, until we say, "I heard a sound," there is no sound. We also experience sounds in the absence of actual physical stimulus in our dreams, in our memory, or in the voice we sometimes hear when we read or think.

For the purpose of exploring the expressive and emotional qualities of musical performance, we will only focus on the purely human experience of sound, not the sound that can be detected only by scientific instruments.

Back to Thor's Story: How Music Was Born

Now of course, Thor knew nothing about music and had no musical skill as we now define it. But Thor did have the ability to push on some keys, and he experienced the power of sound and silence from the start. He was instantly captivated. The musical elements of melody, rhythm, dynamic variation, harmony, and articulation were revealed to him. He courted them and fell in love with them. He played a high note that sang clear and crisp and echoed through the silence of the cave. He played a low note that rumbled and disappeared into the dark. He began to use the many elements that sound and silence had to offer. He played short notes, little staccatos that chirped and danced. He played long notes that filled the cave. He played two or three notes at a time, then bunches of notes at a time. He used his fingers, as well as his knuckles and arms, to depress the keys.

The sounds blended, crunched, and rumbled. He played loud, with a fullness that thundered, and then even louder, with a forcefulness that shook the air. His body became involved as he jumped and swayed. He allowed the space to have its fun. He played softly, sweetly, mildly, gently, tenderly, and delicately; sometimes hardly even touching the keys which, in turn, spoke to him from what seemed to be a great distance. He played fast sparkling tones and slow mellow tones. He touched keys and played rhythms at random. His emotion poured into the keys and into the air.

The hypnotic repetitions carried him even more deeply into this experience. He was totally involved and totally enthralled with the experience of the sound and with the power of the silence between the sounds. His awareness was engulfed and he was carried away. Thor knew nothing about music and was just beginning to develop skill, yet he was floating six inches above the floor of the cave in a bubble of joy.

Thor returned to the cave day after day and explored the many opportunities that these musical elements offered. Though Thor knew nothing about music, he was having the time of his life.

And that was the way music was born.

Thor's performance continued. Outside the piano cave, other cave people nearby heard and were amazed by the sounds that Thor sent flying into the air. They were drawn to the source of the sounds. They entered the cave, watched, and listened. They were enchanted by the incredible play of sound and silence. The pops and booms and twirls came at them, both sweet and strong. The different pitches followed each other on a roller coaster of sound and silence, through time and space, as if coming from a distant horizon, building up right into their faces, then disappearing behind them into the unseen horizon. Thor's friends were carried away by this "music" floating around the cave in bubbles of joy. Everyone was having the time of their lives. Thor and his friends and the joyful musical elements lived happily ever after until...

One of Thor's friends came to his senses—pop!— and dropped down to the floor, where he could hear himself think, and cried out, without thinking, "Hey, Thor, that's really great, but play something!"

Pop!...pop...pop, pop...pop, pop, pop! Everyone's bubble popped and everyone now stood with their feet flat on the ground.

"Yeah, Thor!" cried another cave person. "Play something! Play some Folk Music! "No!" exclaimed another in a fake British accent. "Play some Classical Music, because Classical Music is sophisticated." The comments continued. "No, Classical Music is square. Play some Jazz, man. Jazz is cool!" "Heavy Metal! We can groove to Heavy Metal. We can feel that in our bones!" "Hey, dude! How about some Rock 'n' Roll? We can dance to Rock 'n' Roll." "Play some Rap and Hip Hop. That's the happening thing!" "Play some Blues. Blues is the root of all American music!" "Hey, Thor, come on, play some Country Music. Country Music is from the heart." "No! No! Play some Gospel Music. Gospel Music comes right from the soul!" People were shouting left and right, up and down. As everyone shouted over everyone else, a cacophony of opinions filled the room. It went on and on for hours, days, weeks, and months...it went on for years, decades, and centuries. It went on for millennia, right up to today, and will into the future.

And that was the way the Music Critic was born.

But Thor didn't care about the music critics. Thor was having the time of his life. And Thor and all of his joyful musical elements lived happily ever after in every flavor and style of music...even among the music critics.

♪ Cleaning the Slate

The story of Thor starts with a clean slate, one without preconceptions about the world of music. It places Thor in a time before intellectual concepts about music existed; before recordings, radio, television, popular or obscure music styles, music producers, right or wrong approaches, and especially before critics appeared—at least until the very end of the story. Because of this, we can easily visualize a picture of what music performance really is—an intimate relationship between the artist's expression and the art form.

There are at least four freeing ideas that come from Thor's perspective:

1. The real power in music—what draws us, holds our attention, and carries us away—is the play of sound and silence and the musical elements that exist in all the flavors and styles of music.

2. Anyone can play music and be fulfilled. Expression exists at any skill level.

3. Music does not know what is hip and what is sophisticated. It doesn't know what is primitive or what is square. These are only sociopolitical and fashion-based concepts. These elements have nothing to do with the art of music. Certainly, we don't have to allow those concepts to make it even more difficult to experience joy in music.

4. When you truly visualize Thor, you realize that you can actually put your whole self into your own performance and not worry how it comes out—because you know in the long run it is only about what what you put into it.

♪ The Search for a Good Definition of Music

The manner in which we look at music can either make it easier or more difficult to get what we want from our musical performance. Music should not be a burden. Music should be a joy. We can look at music and understand it from a point of view that will be uplifting or from a perspective that will be unpleasant or dry. There are enough challenges in the world that we have no control over. Why take music and make it like everything else? Some of us choose to work very hard at our music and some of us work at it a little at a time. However "serious" we are about our music, the more we infuse joy, excitement, and love into our performance, the more we, our audience, and the world will benefit from it.

Understanding Thor's very pure experience of music is a good place to start. Still, maintaining a healthy perspective in the arts is not easy, and a great deal of positive yet realistic reinforcement can be very helpful.

The Importance of Music in the World

The Value of Our Work

We all know music is magic. It has a tremendous impact and holds a significant position in the world. The general public has an insatiable appetite for music. Businesses use music everywhere to sell and enhance their products and services. Who isn't interested in music and where can't music be found? The world is greedy for it! We hear it in just about every public facility, including elevators, and when we are put on hold on the telephone.

Music is everywhere! People jog to it, work to it, eat to it, wake up to it, and fall asleep to it. It is used for therapy. It calms people down and stirs people up. People spend billions of dollars on recordings and equipment. We even leave the comfort of our warm cozy home and drive downtown in the middle of an ice storm just to pay the $48 or more for a single ticket to witness a live concert. It seems the world just can't get enough music. Music makes you want to dance, it makes you sway, it makes you tap your foot, it brings tears to your eyes, it makes you want to get married, it makes you laugh, and it sticks in your memory like the face of a loved one.

One single sound on an instrument fills a room, and its uplifting quality fills every space in everyone from head to toe. Music permeates our lives. A large percentage of our bodies are made of water. I think we may start out as water, but we end up as music!

Very simply, most music makes us feel good. When we feel good, we are nicer to ourselves and nicer to others; and they in turn are nicer to others. In this way, music makes the world a better place for all of us to live in. Think about this. How long does it take to get over the feeling of anger when someone honks the horn unfairly? And when is it ever fair? When I am driving while in an angry mood, I know I am making others angry. And when I get out of the car feeling angry, I know I might treat someone else unfairly, which might make them angry, and so on. There is quite an extraordinary chain reaction that spreads around the world this way. Music takes the edge off; and when we are nice, the world has a better chance of being nice. You've heard the saying, "Music soothes the savage beast." Martin Luther said, "Music is the art of the prophets, the only art that can calm the agitation of the soul. It is one of the most magnificent and delightful presents God has given us."

When people from one social group or region of the world are enjoying the music from a different social group or region of the world, honor and respect flourish, not just for the artists who are making the music, but also for all those people who are lovers of that particular music. This is just one more way that music makes the world a better place for all of us to live.

A Personal Story about the Unifying Power of Music

The power and the importance of music was made clear to me at a performance in 1969 when I faced a hostile audience at the peak of the "generation gap" conflicts which were so pervasive in our society at that time. My group was about to perform "Three Pieces for Blues Band and Symphony Orchestra" with the New York Philharmonic at Lincoln Center. We walked on stage with our amplifiers, guitars, long hair, vests without shirts, and work boots, and stood against a backdrop of New York Philharmonic "penguins" in tuxedos. The crowd, dressed much the same as the classical musicians on stage with tuxedoes and evening gowns, booed and hissed. Someone later wrote that the "generation gap" that evening was wider than the Grand Canyon. As we began the first movement of the concert, the noise from the overwhelming anger began to subside. On stage, everybody hoped the music would do its work, because the situation was clearly out of our hands.

As the performance progressed, I felt the audience's anger and bitterness dissolving into thin air. Poof! After the concert, the president of the symphony association came up to me and told me we had been given the longest and most intense standing ovation he had ever heard in Lincoln Center. As a young musician, this taught me first-hand how music was indeed the universal language. It not only rises above the power of words, it even rises above the power of ideas to vaporize differences among people.

My Questions

One question always leads to more questions. What is the true essence of music? How can this art form be described? What makes it work the way it does? What attracts us to it? What is it that empowers music? What is it that makes music so beautiful and exciting? How can I get more out of it? What can I do to put more into it? What can I do to express myself more deeply through this form? How can I assure great performances? How can I stay in the "zone" while performing or listening? Why do I always "hit the wall"? How can I enjoy myself more consistently? What about stage fright? What about mistakes? What exactly is the seasoning that is used by the seasoned professional? What is the formula for success? What is success? Do I have to suffer to be an artist? Where does criticism fit in? What relevant purpose does the music critic serve? What is the creative process and what actually happens during it? How can I stay inspired? What is the purpose of music anyway? What is sound and how is it perceived? What is the true relationship between the audience and the performer? How is it possible that I love one form of music and someone else hates that very form?

The importance of music in my own life drove me to dig deep to find the meaningful answers to questions like these. My mind still spins out searching for answers.

There are too many pat answers to these questions, given too casually by teachers, idols, and the music and performance industry at large. There are many elusive responses like, "It's a feel thing." There are also exclusive and unjust remarks like, "You just lack talent." There are dogmatic remarks such as, "That's just the way it's done." There are judgmental presumptions like, "There is good music and there is bad music."

In the search for inspiring answers, I was motivated not just by an esoteric personal drive, but by a belief that there was something more to this amazing art form than what I was being told. I sensed that some revelation in this area would lead me not only to intellectual clarity, philosophical understanding, and psychological benefit, but most importantly, to very practical technical applications. I was right.

 # Thick Mythology

I once heard an interview on public radio with the astronaut, Alan Beam. I thought, "This is a guy that can do anything!" First, he walked on the moon. Then he decided to become a painter. However, guided by a common misconception, he was shocked when he got his first taste of the artist's reality. He shared his newfound wisdom with the radio audience, "The mythology surrounding what it is like to be an artist has nothing to do with what it is really like to be an artist."

The mythology that Alan Beam talks about is pervasive in the world of music. The strong and ongoing tendency to define what is hip, square, or sophisticated superimposes false boundaries between musical possibilities and works to separate artists from their inspiration and people from each other. In this environment, the nonverbal and universal power of music must work that much harder to be the unifying force that is its nature.

Not Nice

One's personal self-expression is swallowed up in mythological preconceptions about music. It seemed like a good idea to find a definition of music that was not prejudiced and did not place limits on expression. I was looking for a verbal point of reference, something that supported me, something I could fall back on.

Let's consider the definition of music in *Webster's New Universal Unabridged Dictionary:*

> *The art and science of combining vocal or instrumental sounds or tones in varying melody, harmony, rhythm, and timbre, especially so as to form structurally complete and emotionally expressive compositions.*

If we accept "structurally complete" as part of the definition, we may have to say that Schubert's Unfinished Symphony is not "music" if someone decides for some reason that it is incomplete structurally. If we accept "emotionally expressive" as a requirement for music, who decides when something is emotionally expressive?

Void of Emotional Expression

Example

There was a nationally syndicated radio show featuring "eclectic music." The producer of the show, someone I admired for his knowledge of music, told me he had listened to a piece of music by a Russian composer and thought it was "an emotionally void waste of time." He decided not to include it on his show. The next day he went to a lecture that, coincidentally, included a discussion about the life of this particular Russian composer. Most members of the composer's family were Holocaust victims. The music he composed was dedicated to them. My friend decided to listen to the composition again and this time found that it was "filled with emotion and passion." I asked my friend, "You mean to say the first time you heard it, it wasn't filled with emotion and passion? And the next time you heard it, all of a sudden, it was filled with emotion and passion?" I believe it was always there. Art with or without the artist is beautiful and emotional. We have heard so many times that "beauty is in the eye of the beholder," if the beholder is willing to see it.

A definition of music that gives us reasons to dislike something takes us in the wrong direction, and besides, it's just not nice. Terms like "structurally complete" or "emotionally expressive" can cloud our reality and obscure inner experiences that fuel expression.

What if we consider a description of music that avoids limitation? This description would be broad and, most importantly, inclusive. It would support any and all performance and composition styles and all musicians.

♪ A Nice Description

Music is based in the relationship of sound and silence. Out of this play between sound and silence arises the ecstatic musical elements we call pitch, melody, harmony, rhythm, articulation, counterpoint, tonal variations and dynamic variation. These ecstatic musical elements exist in nature and are independent of the artist. The sound of the wind rustling through the trees, the spring rain on the pond, the melody of the songbird, the forceful clap of thunder, the hypnotic groove of the cricket in the night, and the gentle counterpoint of the babbling brook against the distant articulations of a squirrel's chattering can soothe the soul and uplift the spirit.

The musician comes along and is enchanted and wholly inspired by nature's music. Armed with a palette of sounds, discovery, invention, and the refinement of musical instruments, his or her music blossoms. One note is produced. The vibrations fill the air with this uplifting quality. The musician reaches further in and offers his or her individuality. With varying levels of inspiration, and with diverse impositions of intent, character, expression, and skill level, the artist uniquely manipulates the joyful musical elements.

With this enchanted enthusiasm, the artist serves the vibrating, pulsating, constantly moving, ever-changing play of sound and silence that is the essence of music. The vibrations fill the artist and the world and every person in it from head to toe with this joyful and sublime dance.

Wow! What a fantastic art form!!!

A definition I would like to submit to Webster's Dictionary:

> *The play of sound and silence that gives birth to many joyful elements (timbre, pitch, rhythm, articulation, melody, harmony, counterpoint, and dynamic variation) as they are experienced flowing through time and space. This experience creates a profoundly uplifting, unifying, and healing art form known as music. The artist, through self-expression, offers 'humanity' and 'individuality' to the art form.*

♪ The Importance of Individuality

In an interview published in the *Chicago Tribune,* Daniel Barenboim, former conductor of the Chicago Symphony Orchestra, once explained why he chose certain players over others.

> *I do not believe in passive high-quality technical playing from orchestra musicians.... I strongly believe that in order to have homogeneity you must have individuality. I do not believe you get more homogeneity by having players who are lacking in personality. You must have the personality as well as the ability and willingness to play with others.*

The widely-accepted myth that Daniel Barenboim dispels is that symphonic playing calls for less individuality. On the contrary, even with the goal of homogeneity in mind, this highly respected conductor, along with many of his colleagues, demands character and individuality from musicians.

Exercise

Think about all your favorite artists. Pick three and visualize them on your own wall of fame. These are some of your most cherished icons in the world of music. Though you honor their skills, their achievements, and their talents, it is their individuality that attracts you. It is Bob Dylan's "Dylan-ness," Mozart's "Mozart-ness," P. Diddy's "Diddy-ness," the Beatles "Beatle-ness," Howlin' Wolf's "Wolf-ness," or John Coltrane's "Coltrane-ness." This is the source of your feeling of intimate connection for those artists we truly love.

 ## Out of the Box

Individuality does not necessarily mean "out of the box" or "unconventional." Individuality can even be an expression of your own deep love for a conventional style or a particular artist. Yet even this approach can't diminish true individuality when it comes with conviction. It is this "pouring out" of uninhibited enthusiasm that expresses natural individuality, whatever the result. "In" or "out" of the box is not important. It is not about the box at all. The box can only get in the way. Individuality is an expression that comes from the natural way your own mind, heart, and body are ordered. And when we flow with this, it connects us in a very effective and deep way to any activity we apply it to.

So listen to your heart and offer what makes you feel good, what is exciting to you, what is interesting to you, and what moves you.

Individuality is an expression that comes from the natural way your own mind, heart, and body are ordered. And when we flow with this, it connects us in a very effective and deep way to any activity we apply it to.

THE CRITIC

♪ The Artist and the Critic

From a tiny place in one's heart
Blossoms an offering.

Its purpose is to uplift,
Not to be forced into the small space
Of another's imagination...

...Like squeezing a tree into a seed.

This little poem covers a lot of territory for me. This was Thor's experience. He performed his music for the sheer joy of it. With or without the critic, Thor and his joyful musical elements lived happily ever after.

The Artist: Creativity

Creativity is an intimate process. It begins with being aware of the beautiful, ecstatic, and powerful energy that lies within. The recognition and experience of this energy is commonly known as inspiration. Ideas or objects are side effects of creativity. Creativity, in line with inspiration and true to the heart, will uplift one's life and the world.

The Critic: The Opinions of Others

Our creativity can be stifled or completely consumed by the opinion of others. The critical mind moves the focus away from the beauty of the creative process and into the world of opinion and fashion. This subdues individuality, dishonors diversity, and intimidates one's inspiration, which is the essence of creativity. We need to have more faith in our own inspiration, our own individuality, and our own creativity.

> *Our most persistent and spectacular efforts are concerned not with the preservation*
> *of what we are but with the building up of an imaginary conception of ourselves in*
> *the opinion of others.*
>
> — Eric Hoffer

Criticism in General

Others' criticism can make us humble. That is a very good thing as long as we don't let it compromise our individuality and pull us away from what inspires us. When someone I love—one who loves me, understands me, and really cares about my work—offers constructive criticism, I think of it as a form of wisdom. I have to consider it, let it settle in, and see where it goes. If it's my boss, of course, I probably need to apply it.

♪ The Ideal Critic

The critic at large has an important role: to find positive things to say about a work of art, to highlight the greatness of art, to never bring people down by bringing a work or an artist down, to support the arts, to encourage people and artists. In this context, the critic helps art to do what it does best—bring people together, uplift them, and make the world a better place for all of us. What a great gig for the art critic.

Clarifying the Terms "Critic" and "Criticism"

In this discussion I use the terms "critic" and "criticism" in the completely negative sense. In other words, criticism is the expounding upon what is "wrong" or "undesirable" in a work. The critical mind only notices and seeks the negative, and is not our friend.

 # What's Not to Like?

Consider these artistic intentions for a particular work. They may be conscious or unconscious. I put them in opposing pairs:

- Soothing–Relaxing–Meditative ....Physically Motivating–Mentally Energizing
- Intellectually Interesting ....Simple
- Fun–Humorous ....Serious–Sad
- Nostalgic–Familiar ....Challenging–Unusual
- Technically Complex and Impressive ....Technically Simple

A composition or performance can include any one or a combination of intentions such as those listed above. To make things even more complex, the listener has specific expectations that may or may not fit with the intention of the composition. As you can see, the performer and listener may be at cross-purposes when it comes to the performance. Perhaps before passing judgment on an artistic work, one should understand the intention of the work. Otherwise we might be criticizing the bird for not sounding like a cat.

Because of these many unknowns, criticism can be very unreliable, so forget about it! The practice of criticism naturally creates a narrowing and less realistic perspective.

Now consider that many critics of expert opinion scorned masters like Mozart and Van Gogh during their lifetime. One might pause to consider the integrity of criticism.

 # Criticizing a Flavor of Ice Cream

When someone asks me if I want some ice cream I don't ask, "What flavor?" I don't even think, "What flavor?" I just say, "Yes!" My heart stops when I hear "ice cream," not because it might be strawberry, chocolate, or vanilla, but because ice cream is sweet, cool, and creamy. Sweet, cool, and creamy is the essential nature of ice cream as it effects the senses—it is what draws us in, holds our attention, and carries us away. I may have my very personal preferences, or I may be pulled to a nostalgic memory of a particular flavor, but it is the sweet, cool, and creamy that really does the trick and makes ice cream the unique experience it is.

It is the same thing with music. If we love jazz or classical or heavy metal or country music, the musical elements are what hold us in the experience. Jazz may push us away and classical may pull us because of our preconceptions, or even our lack of openness. But the real power and joy of any flavor of music, the aspect that really holds us and carries us away, is the experience of the powerful play of sound and silence, and the dance of the musical elements.

By remembering that sound and silence hold the beauty and power of music, we allow self-imposed boundaries between musical form and style to disappear. In this way, we allow the music to carry us away. Why play music if it doesn't carry us away, or at least uplift us a tiny bit? When music is experienced as a natural expression, it becomes the universal language, bringing ideas and people together rather than giving us just one more reason to separate ourselves from each other. The more reasons I can find to be non-critical about music, the better. This helps me focus more positively on my own work.

NON-JUDGMENT

The critical mind, or the inner critic, is very sneaky. Even when we stop criticizing ourselves, it tries to pass itself off as a necessary partner in creativity, something called the judgment process. Let's explore the advantages of non-judgment and see how the judgment process foils our purpose as musicians and performers.

People commonly believe that judgment is an important part of the creative process. I associate judgment with critical thinking and know that critical thinking is never a good thing in the arts. Knowing the difference between judging and making choices is extremely important for an artist for many reasons.

Please think about the following everyday experiences that illustrate the creative process and the practice of non-judgment. Then we will examine a creative method for making choices that can replace the judgment process.

The Beginner's Advantage

I once taught some children how to play a paddleball game. I knew from my tennis lessons that focusing on the ball is essential. I told the children to just focus on the ball so hard that everything else would be a blur. We had a good time hitting the ball back and forth with mostly long volleys. Their dad wanted to try it. He had some experience playing tennis and asked me how he should hold the paddle. I told him not to think about how he was holding the paddle, just focus on the ball. He then said he didn't know how to hit a backhand with this paddle and didn't know if he should turn his body or face forward. I told him to just focus on the ball. We never got a decent volley going. The children didn't have much practice at paddleball, and they didn't have much practice being judgmental either. So they were pretty good at playing paddleball.

Welcome to the judgment process. This is the critical mind. It can be crippling. If we practice it, we get good at it, and it becomes habit.

Think about beginner's luck in sports such as bowling, darts, golf, and baseball. Once, a fellow who used to watch baseball games at the park was asked to stand in for a batter. He never played baseball before, but he hit a home run. The team asked him to play every week, so he joined the team. He struck out every time at bat after that.

My wife, Holly, was casually playing darts with some friends. It was her first time playing darts and she was hitting very well. She even hit the bulls-eye a couple times. Her friends then chose teams. She couldn't hit anywhere on the target after that. The housepets were in danger!

Wouldn't it be great if we could take whatever quality exists during beginner's luck and apply it to everything we do? We can! One of the qualities required to reproduce beginner's luck is "non-judgment." It is one's ability to leave the critical mind out of the process. Many people who play sports know this.

Goals or the focus on results will often activate the critical mind. A beginner has little invested, little knowledge, and therefore little need to make judgements. The mind bypasses the judgment zone and connects directly to the action. Now we are working at our highest potential—bulls-eye!

Creative Energy: The Oh, Ooooh, Ah! Experience

Sometimes the harder you try to remember the name of a movie, the more difficult the process becomes. When you finally give up trying, all of a sudden the name appears.

Just before you realize that the name is about to come up you feel this sweet burst of energy. I call this the "Oh" experience.

"Oh"

In the second part of this instant you become aware of the name of the movie. The great feeling that accompanies this is called the "Ooooh" experience.

"Ooooh"

Then the name just pops out of nowhere and you say it: "An Affair to Remember!" This feeling you experience just as you begin to speak the name is called the "Ah" experience.

"Ah"

Taken together, this experience is the flow of creative energy. It is what we call inspiration.

"Oh—Ooooh—Ah"

Intuition is the directing aspect of inspiration. The power of inspiration and intuition can take us a long way, even with limited skills. This mental state and its application increase skill and make good use of the skills we currently have. That's the power behind beginner's luck. When people talk about working from the heart, they are really talking about bypassing the critical mind and going right for the action. Inherently people know this.

All of the classic statements about playing music from the heart—getting into the zone, getting out of the way of the music, being a conduit for the music, forgetting everything you know, getting into the groove—mean the same thing: get the critical mind out of the way and allow inspiration to have its day.

Intuitive Differentiation

Thor convinced us that our job description as artists is to create an environment for inspiration to flow, to stay focused on the task, to follow our intuition, and to enjoy the individual expression that comes out. Of course you can make choices. You can make choices through the judgment process (via the critical mind), sorting through pros and cons, accepting "the good" while rejecting "the bad." I believe the judgment process interrupts the flow of creative energy in many ways. So how can we make choices without using judgment?

Another way of making choices comes from accepting what feels good and letting everything else just dissolve without stopping to examine it. This is called intuitive differentiation. We use the nonintellectual, nonverbal experience of intuition as it is fueled by inspiration. This allows us to distinguish between choices. In this way, the deep, powerful, and pure aspect of our natural makeup becomes the director. The result is a powerful expression that is "us," not a compromise or projection of someone's opinion. This is our individuality in action. With intuitive differentiation we are deeply connected to our choices in a profound way.

Composing with Intuitive Differentiation

In the process of composing, for instance, an idea comes and you see how it feels. Does it fit with your feeling of inspiration? If it does, you write it down. If it doesn't, you just let it go. And you can re-examine your decisions by applying trial and error to see if it still feels good—without getting caught up in judgment.

Rehearsing with Intuitive Differentiation

In a rehearsal with a group or an ensemble you try a piece one way, then you try it another way, and then you try it the first way again. No discussion is necessary; you choose the one that feels good. Rehearsals conducted this way are much more enjoyable and keep the group on track.

This is a great way to make artistic choices and stay connected to your natural self—your powerhouse of pure expression.

Performing with Intuitive Differentiation

In performance, everything happens so fast that you are forced into intuitive differentiation, at least to some degree. In fact, performing actually teaches us to use intuitive differentiation and practice non-judgment. You are "going with the flow," caught up in the moment, and experiencing a beautiful feeling.

A note of caution: if we use intuitive differentiation to make a choice, and then think, "I like that!" we head right back to the judgment process. When you notice how great your idea was, it works much better to say, "Thank you," and move on.

Fearlessness—The Secret Tool

Fearlessness is a secret tool that allows us to follow our inspiration and practice non-judgment. Fearlessness allows us to operate at peak performance and it connects us to the action in the moment. It allows creativity and individuality to flow and helps us recognize a great discovery as it passes in front of us.

Exploration and experimentation is part of our job as artists. It is the "artistic way" to look for alternatives and explore the territory beyond what is safe, comfortable, and known.

Exercise

Imagine that you are playing the piano in front of 3,000 people. The tempo is quarter note = 120 beats per minute in marching time, but you are playing mostly eighth notes. In other words, you are flying. Every tick of the clock you play four notes. Whew! Fast! (This is the same tempo as "Stars and Stripes Forever.") This performance demands your focus. If you are in the habit of using the judgment process, you can't just shut it off, especially when you make a mistake.

Imagine that you make a mistake. You recognize the mistake but you do not want to take your focus off the moment. Dwelling on past events is the antithesis of where your focus should be at a precarious time like this. If you wince or react or put even the slightest attention into this you are focusing on a past event, while the more vital and essential event, the present event, goes unnoticed and continues to happen without your full blessing. A delicate balance has been disturbed. This leads to even more mistakes, a possible complete shut down. At the very least, it causes you to miss what could have been the peak experience we musicians all love to talk about.

The judgment process focuses on what has transpired, which is the past. Intuitive differentiation is the experience of the moment and keeps you focused on the present.

One student I coached had been studying violin for about six months. She made faces every time she hit a "wrong" note and said, "Sorry" or "Oops" or "Yuck." I went up to the music and began examining it. She wanted to know what I was looking for. I told her I was looking to see where "Oops" or "Yuck" was written in the music. We both had a good laugh and then I asked her to place her violin on the couch and pluck a string. I asked her to note how beautiful that sounded. I then asked her to drag her bow across the strings and note how the sound filled the room with such a pleasant and uplifting quality. Practicing non-judgment, I asked, "How could there be a wrong note?" The purpose was to get her to stop being interrupted by the wrong notes and to move her out of the judgment process that was partially responsible for the wrong notes in the first place! Of course, you work for the "right note," but not at the cost of losing touch with the beauty of the music.

Why Be Afraid of Mistakes?

The psychological state of never being satisfied for the sake of advancement actually prevents advancement. Worse, it instills fear, distorts our perception, and sabotages the reason we play music in the first place. Trying to assure that mistakes won't happen is folly. Mistakes are often just spontaneity in action. Lack of spontaneity can be a bigger problem. Though we can work toward illusory perfection, at the same time we need to accept what we have and stay in touch with its beauty and its "perfection up to now." This is non-judgment.

Part Two
An Introduction to the
World of Dynamic Variation

Dynamic variation, or dynamics, is commonly known as the variation or the changing in volume between loud and soft. Experiencing degrees of sound and silence puts us in touch with the power of music. Dynamic variation brings musical performance to life in many surprising ways. Understanding dynamic variation, its benefits and how it works, is an excellent foundation for taking advantage of music's gifts when practicing, performing, or teaching others.

WHAT DYNAMICS DOES AND HOW IT WORKS

 ## Three-Dimensional Quality

Dynamic variation transforms music from a two-dimensional to a three-dimensional experience. If we were to visualize the different musical elements in space, we would tend to do it the way it looks on the staff, printed on a two-dimensional plane, like this page.

Pitch:
Higher and lower pitch is perceived as moving vertically, up or down on the plane, the same way it is written on the musical page.

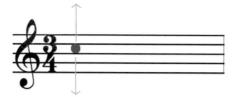

Harmony:
Two or more pitches sounded at the same time result in what we call harmony. We perceive harmony in much the same way as pitch: higher and lower, portrayed on a vertical line on the plane.

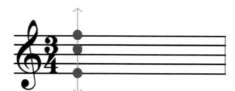

Harmonics:
When a particular pitch is played on an instrument, there are actually many other, less audible pitches (mostly higher) generated at the same time— harmonics. The higher ones are treble pitches; the lower ones are bass pitches. The more these harmonic pitches can be heard, the more they affect tonal quality. This is much like harmony and can also be perceived on a vertical line on the plane, either higher or lower.

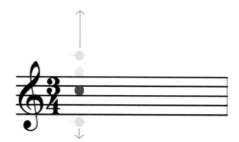

We tend to perceive musical time as moving horizontally across a plane from left to right. This is also how it is represented on a musical page. The notation I will be using for the following illustrations are visually clearer than normal rhythmic notation.

Normal rhythmic notation
Notes and rests (spaces) can be perceived moving through time on a plane from left to right.

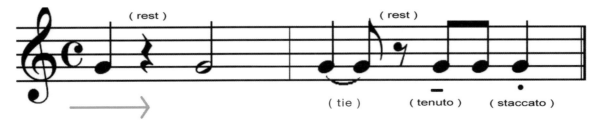

Notation to visually represent duration
Duration, articulation, space, and rythmn, symbolized on this page, represent the second dimension of the musical form.

These three elements of music are associated with time:

Duration: Notes and rests (spaces) moving from left to right. Notes and rests can have longer or shorter durations. (See illustration above.)

Articulation: This is essentially the same as duration. The staccato shortens notes and the tenuto lengthens notes. The tie bridges two notes together so that they become one note without any space in between. Most articulations are related to the length or the duration of a given sound. Therefore, I place the element of articulation into this horizontal plane (see the illustration above).

Rhythm: The series of sounds, with spaces in between, runs through time and results in "rhythm." Imagine a rhythm running across your room from left to right along an imaginary horizontal path. (See illustration above.)

Duration, articulation, space, and rhythm represent the second dimension of the musical form.

Exercise

Picture a beautiful two-dimensional form of music dancing in front of you on an invisible flat surface. We can hear and see melodies, harmonies, and all of the other elements of music moving up and down, left to right. What joy! Now picture a musical pitch (as a small dot) way behind the surface, all alone in the distance, one you can barely see or hear.

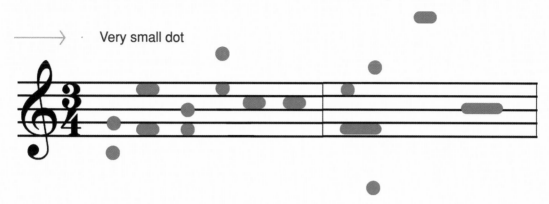

Very small dot

Very smoothly, but quickly, this dot moves toward you, creating a crescendo at the same time. It gets larger and louder until it moves right through the invisible flat surface and up to your face.

Very small dot

Adding the element of dynamic variation into the mix transforms the music from two dimensions to three dimensions, creating an auditory "holographic" experience. We will also mark the dynamics below with traditional marks to show *"p"* for piano in Italian, which means soft; *"f"* for forte, which means loud; and *"mf,"* for mezzo forte, which means not so loud.

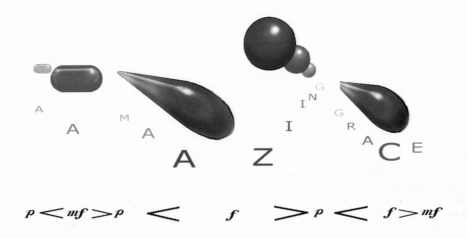

From Expansive to Intimate Qualities

When you speak loudly in most rooms, you can hear the sound of your own voice reverberating off the walls. To the listener, the main sound source is you, but it is mixed in with the reverberations bouncing off the walls and other surfaces. The reverberations fill the room with sound and create a sense of expansiveness. If you speak very quietly, the sound no longer reaches the walls. The multiple sound sources disappear, and the listener experiences only the very intimate sound coming directly from you. When you apply dynamic variation to music, this same powerful fluctuation occurs to create the contrasts between expansive and intimate experiences. Very exciting.

Emotional Qualities

In the following diagram, the left side lists the basic degrees of a dynamic range described with the sense of hearing in mind, from soft to loud. Listed on the right are the basic physical versions of the same range, from very delicate to forceful. The elements on the right connect more directly with the physical act of playing music. I believe this points out the emotional possibilities that exist in a spectrum of dynamic possibility.

Hearing/Listening Qualities	Performance Qualities
Intellectual Qualities	Emotional or Physical Qualities
Very soft	Very Delicate
Soft	Delicate
Not so soft	Mild
Not so loud	Full
Loud	Strong
Very loud	Forceful

♩ Spectrum of Emotional Qualities

The purpose of the following diagram is to show how each intensity level from delicate to forceful, **pp** (the Italian notation for *pianissimo*, which means very soft), to **ff**, (the Italian notation for *fortissimo*, which means very loud), offers special expressive and emotional properties. Using only a couple levels, mild to full for instance, leaves out many possibilities which can add expression, contrast, character, and intensity to a performance.

Traditional Notation	Intensity Levels: Expressive Synonyms

pp   Very Delicate to Extremely Delicate: murmur, hint, trace, secret, concealed, seductive, private, secluded, feeble, motionless, fragrant, subtle, fragile, careful, supple, submissive, meek, shy, cautious, sly, removed, distant, unapproachable, introverted, still, susceptible

p   *Delicate: gentle, light, kind, sensitive, polite, patient, soothing, agreeable, sweet, soft, malleable, yielding, amiable, courteous, fair, peaceful, agreeable, tame, considerate*

mp   Mild: moderate, calm, temperate, modest, cool, reasonable, mellow, willing

mf   FULL: READY, SOLID, UNFOLDING, OPEN, PRESENT, HEALTHY

f   STRONG: hardy, robust, vigorous, energetic, convincing, effective, heavy, reverberant, big, hearty, enthusiastic, zealous, direct, assertive, confident, enthusiastic, deliberate

ff   FORCEFUL: POWERFUL, MIGHTY, HEALTHY, INTENSE, TREMENDOUS, RESOUNDING, THUNDEROUS, AGGRESSIVE, MASSIVE, UNINHIBITED, RAMBUNCTIOUS, STORMY, HUGE, EXCITING, THRILLING, ROUSING, EXHILARATING, UNTAMED, FEROCIOUS, UNRESTRAINED, WILD, CRAZY!

♪ Richness in Tone

Through continued experimentation with microphone techniques for my Chamber Blues group, I've discovered that the violin produces many sounds, some beautiful, and some very ugly. Place the microphone over one spot of the violin and you hear a very round and smooth tone. Move the microphone one inch away, and that tone becomes an almost complete distortion, like the sound of a man clearing his throat. The sound of the violin is generated by a combination of sounds with a spectrum of qualities—not all of them desirable when standing alone, but beautiful when they combine.

When you play delicately on your instrument, the sound might be thin or scratchy. When you play forcefully, it may sound a little distorted. Although less desirable as stand-alone sounds, touching upon these extremes totally improves the "richness" of the tone; something that just won't happen otherwise. This richness is generated automatically when dynamic variation is applied. You will notice this when you compare the static and dynamic versions of the audio examples in the audio CD.

♪ Technical Advantage

When your muscles work at one intensity for a long period of time, they become rigid. When your muscles are kept flexible through varying physical intensities, many aspects of your technical abilities improve. First attempts at intensity variation can compromise control and accuracy. But after only a few minutes, you will not only catch up to your normal technical comfort level, but surpass it—and you will be playing dynamically!

♪ Rhythm

Using a larger dynamic range, and especially increasing the delicate side of it, produces many more contrasting accents that increase the "drive" of the rhythm. Also, the flow of dynamics opens up creativity and rhythmic spontaneity, which also add to the groove.

♪ The Sweet Spot

Tennis players refer to the "sweet spot," where the ball hits a particular area on the strings of the racquet, producing a "perfect feel." The response and accuracy feel "sweet." Musical instruments also appear to have "sweet spots," where the right amount of pressure and force feels good and offers the best tonal response and technical control. But over time, this sweet spot becomes elusive. You often find that you need to play a tiny bit stronger than normal, or a tiny bit more delicately than normal, to get that perfect, desirable feel and tone. The fact is, the real sweet spot on a musical instrument is not a spot at all. It is the instrument's dynamic range that offers you the sweetest feel, the richest tone, and the most accurate technical control.

INTENSITY VARIATION

♪ It's About Feel

I ask students in my workshops to focus deeply on the physical act of playing, with particular attention to varying their physical intensity from delicate to forceful. Intensity variation is what produces sonic, or dynamic variation. Since it is a physical activity, it is much more important to pay attention to "the feel" rather than "the sound." I find that when students focus on intensity variation, their playing improves quickly, and dramatically. This section on Intensity Variation includes theoretical ideas about why this works so well, and brings to the forefront some of the more unconscious joys of music performance.

As we have seen, traditionally the dynamic range is notated by symbols that represent the possibilities between *loud* and *soft*:

1. *pp*   (pianissimo/very soft)
2. *p*   (piano/soft)
3. *mp*   (mezzo piano/not so soft)
4. *mf* (mezzo forte/not so loud)
5. *f* (forte/loud)
6. *ff* (fortissimo/very loud)

These terms relate to the sense of hearing more than any other sensory experience. Therefore, they connect more directly to the activity of listening than to the activity of playing.

♪ An Overview of the Ten Factors in a Musical Moment

Consider the chronology of a single moment of music performance:

1. Intention
2. Motion of Preparation
3. Motion of Follow Through
4. Pressure
5. Kinesthetic Experience (the electrical flow between muscle and brain)
6. Touch Experience
7. Physical Vibration Experience
8. Vibrating Air
9. Hearing/Listening
10. Reverberation

Steps 1-4 are under the artist's immediate control. Steps 5-7 are a "result" of the artist's intention and action. Though a great source of intimacy, inspiration, and joy between the artist and the instrument, these very noteworthy factors are not "in charge" of the performance. Steps 8-10 are passive, since they happen after the artist's emotional and physical input. Let's look at this more closely.

♪ The Controlling Factors

1. Intention

Intention happens before a string is struck, a key pressed, or air pushed through reeds or vocal chords, and it continues throughout the performance. To a large extent it pervades all the other steps in playing music. Intention happens—whether intended or not. Intention relates to what we normally call "emotion" in a performance. We don't actually need to divide emotions into categories such as sad or happy. Emotion is simply expressive energy. The energy behind emotion is our intention. If we energize our intention we won't have to worry about emotion—it will just happen. Intention gives your musical performance profound feeling.

It might be our inner expression directing our total performance, or it may be our different levels of intensity directed toward each and every note. Intention can be conscious or unconscious. If you are not consciously aware of your intention toward all the notes of a speedy scale, it is still happening at a subconscious level. Intention is directly connected to the heart, the place of inspiration, and therefore it is connected to the natural expression of the artist at any skill level.

Intention, conscious or unconscious, is communicated through your nervous system to the muscles. These actions contain enormous expressive qualities.

We have a choice. We can just let our intention happen, or we can put our enthusiasm, joy, and heart into it. In other words, we can run on autopilot, or we can infuse each tone with our own expression. Don't wait for your music to bring joy to you; inject your joy into your music. Intention inspires action. The essential components of action are preparation, motion, and pressure.

2. Motion of Preparation

The motion of preparation begins when you set out to play the first tone. The motion of preparation may include taking a breath to sing or blow into a wind instrument; or lifting, shifting, or placing the hands or fingers on an instrument. This motion of preparation contains a great degree of feeling and expression for the artist, yet not a single sound has been produced. This preparation does not stop after the first tone. Silent micro-preparations continue throughout the performance, even after the sound is produced by the voice or instrument.

3. Motion of Follow-Through

Preparation is followed by physical momentum, including the downward motion of the hands and fingers on keyboards and strings, the direction of the bow, the fingering of a wind instrument, forming the words, or the pulling away of the tongue on the reed. All these motions and micro-motions carry expressive energy.

4. Pressure

Pressure is the squeezing motion of the muscles for controlling the instrument or the voice in various ways.

♩ Instantaneous Experience Factors

5. Kinesthetic Experience

The sensation of kinesthetic energy immediately follows motion and pressure. Kinesthetic energy, the electrical energy flowing through the nervous system to the brain, is produced by muscle activation. Kinesthetic experience is the first "monitor" for the controlling factors in music. It happens first, before a sound is produced, and affects every aspect of performance. This physical connection allows musicians to tap directly into their emotions during music performance.

Our muscular motions during performance also create rhythmic feedback signals that keep our body in sync with the rhythm of the music. Tapping our feet or bobbing our heads, for instance, helps us hold a tighter rhythm.

6. Touch Experience

The experience of touching or playing an instrument is different from the kinesthetic experience. Like the kinesthetic experience, it is immediate. However, it is caused by the stimulation of the nerve endings on and near the surface of the fingers, hands and lips as the instrument is played, rather than by muscle activation.

7. Physical Vibration

Plucking a string, striking a key or a drum; sending breath through the vocal chords, lips, a mouthpiece or a reed; all of these actions cause vibrations. These physical vibrations are instantly communicated directly through the musician's body, not through the air. They create an intimate and immediate connection to the musician's intentions and actions.

♩ The Passive Factors

8. Vibrating Air

When the instrument is set to vibrating, the air molecules around the instrument vibrate. A chain reaction sends these vibrations out through the air in all directions.

9. Hearing/Listening

Eventually, these vibrations make it to the ear only after they have traveled through the air, where they are translated into electrical energy and then finally experienced as sound. You can also feel vibrations with your body, in addition to hearing them through your ears, but we consider all of this as the hearing experience.

10. Reverberation

Vibrations that travel through the air and "bounce around the room" eventually reach the musician's ears and add dimension to the initial hearing experience. This bouncing around of the sound is called reverberation.

♪ Air Guitar

Exercise

Try playing the "air guitar." Pretend that you are picking up (or sitting down with) your instrument. Now pretend that you are playing it (or singing). But don't make a sound. Put all of your emotional intention into this silent performance and include all the physical motions. All of the emotion and excitement (if you put them in) should be felt as if you are really playing—but without the sound. This illustrates the degree to which sound is NOT the most important aspect for experiencing emotion in your own performance.

When people tap rhythms, even silently, to an imaginary tune, it is not for the sound but for the "feel" of the rhythm, in other words, for the kinesthetic and touch experience. One can have an expressive experience playing a practice keyboard that makes no sound, playing a practice pad instead of a snare drum, or playing the air violin or air guitar. When I write music, I often click my tongue on the roof of my mouth and imagine I am playing the various parts on various instruments. This way, I can actually "feel" how it is going to feel in a live performance.

Watching "The Musician's Dance" on Television

Turn on the television and look for a show featuring classical musicians. If you can't find classical musicians, find any musicians on the television who are not dancing. Traditionally classical musicians don't dance when they play. Turn down the volume and you will see that even though the musicians may not appear to be "dancing" at first, there is a dance going on. Fingers are flying in speedy rhythm, hands are flailing, bodies are swaying, feet are tapping or wiggling, heads are bobbing, shoulders are twitching, eyebrows are bouncing. What we don't see is the more subtle but constant dance of the tension and release of the necessary muscles, or the kinesthetic energy coming back at them from this dance. The sound on the television is off, yet you can see, even with this limited view, much of the expression the musicians are pouring into their instruments to create a sonic experience.

It is not that sound is unimportant; it is ultimately important. However, if your goal is a perfect sonic performance, you must still focus on some aspect of the dance that controls the sonic output.

Focus and Terminology

We will focus mostly on intention, motion, and pressure, rather than the more passive hearing/listening concepts. We will also define the dynamic range with terms that relate more to intention, motion and pressure, rather than using terms that define the more passive hearing/listening terminology.

♪ The Emotional Connection

Emotional expression is an inner experience. Since it is such an intimate and personal thing, can someone really "teach" someone else how to express emotion? I believe you cannot teach emotion. The good news is that everyone has the ability to express themselves even more deeply than they can imagine. Although emotion cannot be taught, it can be ignited in just about anybody. By helping someone, or yourself, suspend concern about the sound when singing or playing an instrument and focusing instead on touch and feel, emotions come pouring out—and the sound improves anyway!

The Audition

Many years ago, while auditioning string players for Chamber Blues, I heard about a musician whom no one was recommending. I spoke with several conductors who knew the player, and all of them told me this person had great chops but played with no emotion. I decided that "no emotion" was easy to fix as long as this person had the chops that were needed. At the audition, the player walked in, sat down, and began playing with almost no apparent emotion. I stopped him and asked if it would be OK for me to coach him for five minutes and have him come back another time to complete the audition. The player took the coaching, came back later, and blew everyone else away. At this player's first performance, the conductors I consulted earlier asked what I "did" to this person.

What I "did" to this person was focus him on an aspect of his playing that put him in control of his performance. For example, if a baseball batter focuses on the players in the field to see where he should direct the hit, he will very likely miss the ball. If he focuses very intently on the ball, not only will this ensure a connection, but also all the other elements of his swing will fall together naturally, as well as the knowledge of where to direct the hit. Similarly for musicians, focusing on "the controlling factors" not only supports technique and tone but also connects the players with their emotions.

♪ The Revised Language of Dynamics

The following is a revised dynamic range for contemplation and exploration. The terms are designed to be less intellectual and more tactile:

ø	=	*niente*/nothing
ppp	=	extremely delicate
pp	=	very delicate
p	=	delicate
mp	=	mild
mf	=	full
f	=	strong
ff	=	forceful

If you let this revised language of dynamics guide you, and develop these skills, they will connect your emotions to the controlling factors of music performance and you will see amazing results.

THE LISTENING SECTION

About Listening

Listening to the samples on the accompanying CD should be very helpful. Before you listen to these examples, let me share an experience with you.

Many years ago, I found myself in a very challenging situation. We were recording vocal and harmonica overdubs onto previously recorded rhythm tracks made during one of my solo projects. (These cuts can be heard on the compilation CD, *Solo Flight*.) The session did not go well. I tried for eight hours to get the parts right. The producer was upset and thought nothing was usable. The engineering crew would not even look at me. The eight-hour-plus session felt like a total waste. After cooling off for six months, I went back into the studio to finish the overdubs, recorded everything in three takes, and went home to study the tapes and choose the best and most expressive performances. Although the session went amazingly well, I asked the engineer for the takes from the first session, just for comparison. You won't believe it—I swear it is completely true—every single take from that horrible eight-hour session was much better than the re-done tracks. When you listen to *Solo Flight,* what you hear are those original tracks we all thought were not acceptable from the horrible session. Because of this experience, I changed my methods for choosing tracks.

As performers, it would be most efficient to be completely in "performance" mode while performing or recording, and delve deeply into "listening" mode when making decisions. When we record, and we know the performance will be immediately reviewed, subtle psychological distractions compromise our performance potential. The same is true of listening. Therefore you may want to consider allowing the two modes to remain completely separate from each other—both physically and mentally. Close and comparative listening, separated from the performance, is an easy way to remove the moods that can interfere with an objective decision-making process.

Please listen closely to the recorded examples on the CD that accompany this book. Don't just listen to each example once; listen a few times. The first time, listen for technical perfection, the second time listen for emotion, the third time listen for feel. Use intuitive differentiation (see page 31) and notice how each listening session makes you feel. You will uncover many secrets.

And, when you record your own experiments, give yourself at least a day off before comparing your takes to each other.

Audio Examples and Illustrations

The following explanations, illustrations and examples will familiarize you with the choices offered by dynamic variation. You can hear for yourself how dynamics, in many ways, affects the emotional and musical quality of a performance. This will provide a foundation and help you get the most out of the exercises. Listen carefully.

For the sake of comparison, each set of examples is in one key, and in one tempo. This will make it easier to see and hear how the application of dynamic variation, without the help of other variations, can create different effects.

The musicians exercised a certain amount of spontaneity while recording these examples. Therefore, what you hear may differ slightly from what is notated on each specific track.

As you listen to the audio examples on the CD, keep asking yourself these important questions: How does it feel? Which versions have more of the positive qualities listed in the "important questions" below? Are these the qualities I want to experience and share in my musical performance?

Track 1: Introduction and Various Examples

In order to experience the essential subtleties, make sure you are listening in a quiet environment or using earphones and have the volume level up so it feels like the musicians are right there in the room with you.

♪ No Dynamics—Some Dynamics—More Dynamics

Tracks 2, 3, & 4: Chamber Music

Use your remote so you can jump around among Tracks 2, 3, and 4. Make your own comparisons between the three tracks. Study each track several times and notice how your experience deepens and changes.

♪ The Important Questions

Based entirely on your own feeling, which version is more...

1. Emotional and expressive?
2. Passionate?
3. Moving?
4. Exciting?
5. Compelling?
6. Effective?
7. Intimate?
8. Inviting?
9. Interesting?
10. Colorful?
11. Dimensional?
12. Rich in tonal quality?
13. Fun?
14. Joyful?
15. Uplifting?
16. Individualistic and filled with character?
17. Adventurous?
18. Spontaneous?
19. Musical?
20. Artistic?
21. Masterful?
22. Interactive between the musicians?
23. Interactive between the musicians and listener?

You may add to the list any additional positive qualities you find useful.

Track 5: Cross Dynamics—Chamber Music

Now listen to this example of **Cross Dynamics**. Compare this track to the other tracks, especially Track 2 (**No Dynamics**), and respond again to the list of qualities opposite.

Notes and Comments on Tracks 2 Through 5

Track 2: No Dynamics

In the chamber music performance of Track 2, the sound is lush, with an emotional quality. The overall experience is satisfying, beautiful and uplifting. The musicians do not vary the dynamics much on this track.

Track 3: Some Dynamics

In this example, the only aspect of the performance that changed is the addition of some strong dynamic variation.

Track 4: More Dynamics

Here the musicians exaggerate the already exaggerated written dynamics.

Notice the first *ff* ("forceful") in the first measure of the score above. In the recording you will hear that the forceful intensity happens only for a split second. This is because the violinist crescendos quickly from a *pp* ("very delicate") and as soon as he reaches *ff*, he immediately begins the short decrescendo back to *pp*. This dynamic treatment reduces the sonic effect of the *ff* to an *f* ("strong"), or even a little less because the full effect of the "*ff*" never quite has time to get established. You can still feel a special energy without it destroying the musical flow or sweetness of the piece, which could happen with a direct jump from a *pp* to *ff*, or with an *ff* that lasts for a few seconds. Preceding an *ff* with a quick crescendo and immediately following with a quick decrescendo can be a very practical use of extreme dynamics.

In the reverse version of this, when a *pp* is approached by a quick decrescendo and followed by a quick crescendo, the effect of the *pp* can be obliterated. A *pp* is rarely disruptive to musical flow, so the general rule is, in order to have an effective *pp* section, you must allow *pp* to establish itself for at least one second. In the second measure of the score, you can see a *pp* followed by a *ppp*. You need even more time for the "extremely delicate" effect to establish itself, and therefore come through in the performance.

The dynamic treatment that uses quick crescendos and decrescendos will be discussed in a simpler manner beginning on page 53 (see "The Wiggles: Phrasing, Flow, and Micro-Dynamics").

Cross Dynamics—A Closer Look

Cross dynamics denotes one line of music moving dynamically in a crescendo against another line which is simultaneously moving dynamically in a decrescendo. Cross dynamics provides a surprisingly wonderful experience and fantastic musicality.

The Unique Effect of Cross Dynamics

Track 5: Cross Dynamics

As you listen to Track 5, you may notice that the constant crossing of dynamics produces the effect of one overall dynamic level. You may also notice that due to all the dynamic counterpoint, a powerful emotional churning effect results. The joy and character of each part are in full effect; the parts are illuminated, not buried.

Applying cross dynamics opens yet another pathway to expression, creativity, and spontaneity. When ensemble players improvise their dynamics within a wide range, cross dynamics naturally occurs in addition to the normal unison dynamics of ensemble playing. If players must follow a strict dynamic plan (such as in a classical composition) cross dynamics can be superimposed with subtlety as a natural flow of self-expression. This approach offers beautiful results and is a very fun technique to use!

Go back to Track 2 and then compare it to Track 5. Then compare Tracks 2 through 5.

♪ Block Dynamics

I've chosen "Amazing Grace" for my instructional example because it is a simple, well-known, and much-loved melody. A slave-ship captain, faced with his demise in a raging storm at sea, wrote "Amazing Grace." During a flash of inspiration, he awakened to the wickedness of his own deeds and experienced a major transformation. I have always loved this song, but I never understood the words "a wretch like me" until I read the story I mention above.

Our singer is Marcy Levy, also known as Marcella Detroit. She is known for writing and singing "Lay Down Sally" with Eric Clapton, with whom she toured for seven years. Marcy also toured with Leon Russell, performed as a soloist on the Duets *album with Elton John, and performed with Aretha Franklin and many other musicians throughout her career. Her own group, Shakespeare's Sister, had a major hit recording that reached the top of the charts in England.*

Track 6: AMAZING GRACE—No Dynamics

The following music notation illustration represents Track 6. There are no dynamic markings written into the score other than "***mf***" (*mezzo forte*—not so loud). Marcy sings this beautifully, even though she was instructed to sing only what is written, with no dynamics and no ornamentation. Even without the use of dynamics, the music is beautiful—of course, it's Marcy Levy! Listen to Track 6 and watch the score.

51

Track 7: AMAZING GRACE—Block Dynamics

Track 7 uses a very common style of written dynamics. (See the score below.) This very basic form of dynamics is called "block dynamics" because the dynamic changes take place over longer periods or "blocks" of time.

Listen to just the beginning of Track 7 as Marcy drops her dynamic level abruptly from a *mf* to a *pp* (from the full to very delicate ranges), as is written in the score and under the words "how sweet the sound." With that drop in dynamic, you can feel a special pocket of emotion appear. (Listen to the track again.)

Then Marcy begins the crescendo under the words "that saved a wretch like me." As the dynamic begins to increase in intensity, notice that there is a little boost of emotional energy. As the crescendo continues to grow, the emotional quality is sustained throughout the whole phrase.

Listen to the first two lines, from "Amazing Grace how sweet..." up to "...a wretch like me," and then compare that to the same two lines on Track 6. Do you notice the differences?

NOTE: In the line above, "I was blind but now," the crescendo goes from *p* to *f*. However, *mp* and *mf* are still represented in both intention and effect between the starting dynamic and the ending dynamic of the crescendo.

NOTE: When Marcy sings the word "me" at the end of the second line, there is a slight decrescendo toward the end of that held note. This quick change, which takes place in a short period of time, is the first sign of dynamic flow, an element that we will review later.

Now listen to all of Track 7. The third line begins with a decrescendo before "*I once was lost.*" Just as with the crescendo, notice that the emotional quality along the full decrescendo is sustained right up to the delicate landing on the word "*found.*" Take note that the actual emotional intensity increased even though the dynamic level was decreased. At this point, we can begin to hear that it is the change of dynamics from one level to another that creates an emotional effect.

In the last line, "*I was blind but now,*" there is a shorter crescendo which offers up a special spontaneous character of its own, especially when Marcy hits the word "*now*" with force.

At the next to last word, "**I**," at the end of the piece, another quick drop in dynamic level occurs. Again, notice the special pocket of expression. This is followed by an additional short decrescendo to the word "**see**," which deepens and sustains the emotional energy.

This last line, with dynamic changes occurring in shorter durations, creates dynamic phrasing and dynamic flow. The extra emotional value created by a single change in dynamics, coupled with the emotional power of crescendos and decrescendos, illustrates the value of dynamic flow.

Most experienced players understand this concept at some level and naturally use these techniques. If a spontaneous change in dynamic or a spontaneous crescendo produces a desirable effect, it is natural to continue to use dynamic flow. If you are comfortable with technique, pitch, and rhythm, you can focus entirely on expression. But we don't have to wait. We can focus on expression right now!

The Wiggles: Phrasing, Flow, and Micro-Dynamics

Block Dynamics covers larger blocks of dynamic changes, such as jumps from one dynamic level to another, and long crescendos and decrescendos.

Dynamic phrasing is a gentle rising and falling of dynamic levels. Dynamic phrases generally follow the rise and fall of the melodic content, though they don't have to. Dynamic flow is more spontaneous than dynamic phrasing and does not necessarily follow the melodic content.

Dynamic flow includes micro-dynamics, the dynamic changes that occur on a very few notes, such as one-note swells or a quick crescendo or decrescendo between two or three notes. Micro-dynamics can be used in many ways.

Combining dynamic phrasing, flow, and micro-dynamics is like producing waves on a body of water, rising and falling to varying heights and depths. On top of the waves, there can be smaller waves and ripples that constantly move and change. We'll call these the *wiggles*. We can wiggle anything, and any wiggle can be subtle or intense. A gentle *pp* section or a strong *ff* section can be wiggled slightly to create more contrast and energy. More energy can be created by also applying the wiggles within a long block crescendo or decrescendo.

In most cases, if any dynamics are written into a composition, they are block dynamics. On rare occasions, composers may notate micro-dynamics. If there are no dynamic markings, or just a few, this does not mean that the composer wanted the performer to avoid superimposing a dynamic flow.

Dynamic flow has many benefits that you can both hear and feel. It keeps the music flowing and it keeps the muscles relaxed. Dynamic flow offers constant spontaneity, which keeps the musician actively in touch with the emotional experience. It also benefits the balance in an ensemble. Dynamic flow is the experience of "getting out of the way" and letting the muse have its fun.

Though this may seem complex, putting all of this into practice is simple. Young children can do this in minutes—it's very natural. You don't have to "think." You just need to let go and let it happen, like the spontaneity of the waves on the ocean—rolling, jumping, splashing, and shimmering—playing and frolicking.

But first, more details.

The Wiggles Chart

The dynamic changes written in this phrase are charted on the grid below the staff. Note that the flow on the grid follows the dynamic markings and only coincidentally relates to the melodic phrasing. It is the dynamic markings that are represented on the grid. This clearly illustrates the application of dynamic flow, dynamic phrasing, micro-dynamics, and the wiggles. The way it looks is the way it feels. This is the experience of the natural dynamic flow of the musical energy, which always wants to dance.

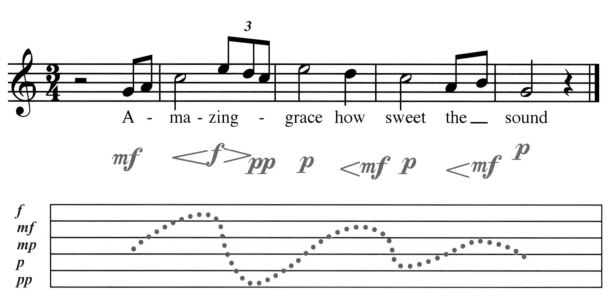

Track 8: AMAZING GRACE—With the Wiggles

In Track 8, Marcy applies the wiggles, constantly varying the dynamics so no two adjacent notes have the same dynamic value. Every note is going somewhere or coming from somewhere dynamically. She did this within as wide a range as possible. The piano also adds some wiggles. The transcribed result of Marcy's performance is in the score below. Listen to Track 8.

Every note should be going somewhere or coming from somewhere dynamically.

In measures two and three in the first line of the score, notice the effect of the micro-dynamics on *"... zing grace."* Also, notice the effects in the middle of the second line on the words *"a wretch."* These little phrases use very extreme dynamics. Compare the dynamic effect of these phrases with the version containing no dynamics on Track 6.

Continuing with Track 8, notice that the general tonal quality is much more rich and diverse. The music jumps out and grabs you, and seems to tell a deeper story. Does it sound to you as if Marcy is more involved and having more fun in this version? A performer must focus intently on using extreme and constant dynamic variation to assure that effective dynamics result. This is because dynamic changes feel more intense to the performer than they sound to the listener.

NOTE: Lyrical content does not necessarily dictate how you approach the dynamic flow. Don't let the lyrics get in the way of your expression. You don't always have to express sweetness on the word *"sweet."* Try it.

By now you may be thinking, "Well, of course there is extra emotion at the dynamic changes, because Marcy is milking the lyrical content." To demonstrate these techniques without lyrics, these next three tracks contain an instrumental version of "Amazing Grace" in the same key and tempo, with the same piano accompaniment. The three examples follow the same structure as the vocal version, i.e., Track 9, no dynamics; Track 10, block dynamics with a dynamic drop and a crescendo; and Track 11, the wiggles.

Track 9: Amazing Grace, Harmonica—No Dynamics

Track 10: Amazing Grace, Harmonica—Block Dynamics

Track 11: Amazing Grace, Harmonica—Wiggles

The following examples are by Michael Miles.

Track 12: Banjo—No Dynamics

Track 13: Banjo—Wiggles

Preparing for the Exploration

It is time to begin your journey through the method and process. The end of this section contains a list of all the steps to follow as you perform the exercises using the method.

 ## The Essential Questions

As I travel around the world giving master classes on dynamic variation, I often begin by asking participants to discuss their most important musical goals. From these discussions, and from my own contemplations, I have compiled a list of essential questions that address most musical goals. This list should look familiar. We asked these questions in the beginning of the "Audio Examples and Illustrations" section, under "THE IMPORTANT QUESTIONS" on page 46. The list includes terms that focus on how we want to feel when we play music, what we want to offer to an audience, and the terms that describe qualities for musicality.

I invite you to review this entire list and decide on a few elements to focus on every time you practice your dynamic variation technique. Please add to the list with each discovery you make.

As you listen or practice, compare the less dynamic versions with the more dynamic versions. Based entirely on your own feeling, ask yourself which version is more...

Emotional and Expressive?	Fun?
Passionate?	Joyful?
Moving?	Uplifting?
Exciting?	
Compelling–Reaches Out and Grabs You?	Individualistic and Filled with Character?
Effective?	Adventurous?
	Spontaneous?
Intimate?	
Inviting?	Musical?
	Artistic?
Interesting?	
Colorful?	Masterful or Impressive?
Dimensional?	
Rich in Tonal Quality?	Interactive between the Musicians?
	Interactive between Musician and Listener?

♩ Coaxing Yourself

Every musician performs on a different instrument or has a distinct vocal range, each with its own set of technical challenges. All musicians, whether professional or student, have a unique performance personality. Most musicians need a lot of coaxing to experience the full benefits of this method. Because I am not here in the room with you, and because I won't get to hear you play or sing, I won't be able to tell you how to make the effective adjustments while you practice this method. You need to do this yourself. In order to do this effectively, you may want to understand some of the "behind the scenes" and fundamental details of this process.

Focus on Intensity Variation

Excellence and true fulfillment have much to do with your ability to focus. The big question for musical performers is "Focus on what?" For the baseball batter, the famous answer is "Keep your eye on the ball!"

There are endless numbers of important things to think about in music performance: pitch, rhythm, time, counting, phrasing, technique, tone, emotion, melody, other players, the articulation, the feel, the conductor, posture. If that isn't bad enough, we think about the audience, mistakes, stage fright, the acoustics, our summer vacation, outside noises, something someone said about us, something someone didn't say about us, and so on.

Just like the baseball speeding toward home plate, the musical moments speed by when we perform. If we pay attention to past moments or other distractions, we miss the musical moments flying at us. Not only will this push us out of the flow, it will cause us to mess up in every possible way.

So if we were to choose only one element of music performance (like the ball in baseball) what would that be? Our logic might tell us to focus on the rhythm and pitch. These are important, but it is your technique—the flow of motion and pressure—that controls rhythm, pitch, and other musical elements. The secret magic potion that makes everything fall into place in musical performance is your focus on intensity variation—the variation of intensity of motion and pressure that results in dynamic variation.

Focus and the Zone

Performing musicians often talk about the occasional feeling of being one with the instrument, being a conduit of universal creativity, being in the zone, being in the flow, being the witness, feeling ecstatic, or feeling inspired. Whatever we call this feeling, it is desirable and healthy. Besides the natural desire to bring joy to others, musicians consider this experience the highest goal of musical performance.

This zone is like the runner's high for an athlete, or the "ah-ha!" experience for a scientist. The zone is not just a great ecstatic feeling, it is a state of mind that allows the artist to operate at the highest level of spontaneity and creativity.

The simplicity of intensity and dynamic variation, and the ease with which you can apply it, makes for an easy pathway to the flowing currents of musical potential. And it is a very effective tool that brings us into the zone. When I work with students and draw their focus to the dynamics, everyone can hear and see the transformation.

When I am in the zone, the focal point is no longer a "point," but an expansive flow of scintillating energy or inspiration, which I associate with a feeling of pure, unqualified, and unattached love.

This experience plays hide-and-seek with me. But I am the one who is hiding. When I focus on my "musical baseball," my dynamic flow and intensity variation, the distractions fade enough for this amazing experience to find me.

Each element of music can be a point of focus and can help bring your musical performance to life. And, you can vary every element of music as an outlet for self-expression. Complete musicality is the artistic variation of all musical elements.

What is different about dynamic variation is that nothing is easier to grasp than the feeling of strong and delicate. Dynamic variation speaks to the essential nature of music—the play of sound and silence. Silence empowers all musical elements and dynamic variation keeps us connected to the power of silence very directly. This becomes a controlling factor on the other musical elements. The variation of each element can be mastered, but if you focus primarily on mastering dynamics, you will reach the heart of musical performance.

♩ Using the Full Range

If dynamics are used at all in performance, it is usually through the use of a small, three-level range of intensity: *mf*, *mp*, and *p*.

A little less common, and more effective, is a four-level range that includes, for example: *f*, *mf*, *mp*, and *p*.

The more uncommon ranges of six and seven levels are the most effective in both projecting and experiencing emotion, excitement, contrast, and sensitivity: *ff*, *f*, *mf*, *mp*, *p*, and *pp* (six levels); or *ff*, *f*, *mf*, *mp*, *p*, *pp*, and *ppp* (seven levels).

Some Cases for Exaggerating Dynamics

The following points will help you gain the confidence to explore the "forceful" and "extremely delicate" ranges without reserve.

- Performers naturally become more focused and physically involved in a performance when dynamics are applied and exaggerated.

- Lang Lang is a popular classical pianist. In response to the critics who say that Lang Lang is prone to exaggeration in his performance, the director of the Chicago Symphony Orchestra, Daniel Barenboim, rebutted with the statement that he "would be very disappointed if Lang Lang wasn't prone to exaggeration."

- Since the early 1990s, my Chamber Blues group has conducted workshops in schools, music academies, and universities around the world. In one of them, I wanted to illustrate the advantages of applying dynamic variation to bring out emotional expression. I asked my string quartet to play a short passage from Mozart, first without dynamics, then with. After they played it both ways, I heard no difference. Two things occurred to me:

    1. The dynamic range used by a performer is usually experienced, by the performer, as much wider than it actually is. Therefore, they avoid truly wide, and effective, ranges because those don't feel right at first.

2. Musicians often have preconceptions and concerns about how historical compositions by acknowledged masters such as Mozart should and should not be played.

During this particular workshop, some members of the group were hesitant to play the Mozart piece with more dynamics than they believed should be applied. I believe this was especially the case in front of an audience of classical music students and professors they may have wished to impress with their mastery of classical repertoire.

I then asked the group to play with extreme dynamics. This sounded good to me, and the audience really responded to the increased emotional quality and improved tonal quality.

Looking for a further demonstration of the power of this simple tool, I asked the group to play with such outrageously extreme dynamics that they would risk ruining the music. The room filled up with beautiful sounds, tonal colors, fluctuations and gorgeous musicality. Everyone in the room seemed transfixed. The audience cheered. The quartet looked very surprised—as do most musicians at a moment like this. Extreme *is* relevant!

In fact, I often find that workshop participants think they are playing in a "too extreme" manner. Most often, the other participants—fellow students and teachers—all agree that they are not playing "extremely" enough!

- When I conduct workshops around the world, people often raise concern about playing with "too much dynamics." I always ask these questions:

  1. How many times do you remember feeling that someone has played with "too much dynamics?"

  2. How many times do you think that a music performance could stand more dynamics?

  3. Is the problem and the challenge about playing with "too little dynamics" or "too much dynamics?"

  4. If the problem is universally "too little," then why are you so worried about "too much?"

- When people start telling you over and over that you play with "too much dynamics," then you should consider mellowing out the top of your range and put extra effort into keeping the changes smooth. It would be a great thing if this happened. "Too much dynamics" is very, very easy to fix. "Not enough dynamics" is harder to fix. The muse offers us a large range for dynamic variation.

It's possible to overdo dynamics, but it's far, far more likely it will be underdone.

♪ Understanding Your Challenge

There are absolutely no occasions in which we would not want the largest possible range of dynamic variation right there at our fingertips, ready for every impulse of inspiration and expression.

To accomplish this, we must fully explore the possibilities that are offered in the extreme ranges, become comfortable with them, and understand them. Then we can make choices from a very large palette of musical and emotional possibility. This is not difficult; it only requires removing your psychological barriers and preconceptions.

At one of my workshops, I was coaching a very competent mandolin player, the last of 15 participants. This is what I asked him:

> *OK, now you know what I am going to ask of you. You saw me do this 14 times so far. So this time, instead of having me guide you into the world of 'delicate,' like I have been doing with the other participants, just play as delicately as humanly possible right now without going through the process. We just heard 14 musicians each try to play as delicately as they could. Each one thought they were playing as delicately as they could, but in fact there were at least three deeper levels attained by just focusing more intently. And the extra levels were really not a technical challenge for any of them. In each case, the added extreme of playing delicately, which was a very useful dynamic, made the performance much more effective, and this was obvious to all of us. So just go for 'extremely delicate' right now, without having me pressure you into doing it.*

I asked him if he thought he could accomplish this and he said, "Yes." He played.

I asked him, "Is that really as delicately as you can play?" And he said, "Yes."

I asked the other players if they thought he could play more delicately. They all nodded. With little effort he then played at a more delicate level.

"Was that difficult?" I asked. He said, "Not really."

"Can you play even more delicately?" I asked. He responded, "I think so."

He played again.

I asked, "Is that really as delicately as you can play?" He answered, "Yes."

I asked the other players, "Can he play more delicately?" They exclaimed, "Yes!" And again he played at a more delicate level. To make a long story shorter, he played through three levels of "more delicate," and when he applied and combined this delicate extreme with the artistic flow of dynamics and the upper extremes, the effect was amazing.

I asked, "Was this difficult?"

He replied, "No, it was easy."

I asked, "Then why couldn't you do it right away?"

It was not a situation where the player couldn't apply the dynamics because of physical limitations. Instead, he was wrestling with a thick cloud of psychology. This psychology challenges you when you explore the ranges of your "forceful" and "delicate" levels. However, it is up to you alone to explore the extremes. We limit our potential by only exploring what we perceive to be possible. We must explore the impossible to know what is truly possible.

Zones of Physical Intensity

On the chart opposite, you can see how far you can explore dynamic variation yourself. Go ahead—break out of your comfort zone!

♪ The Comfort Zone

The comfort zone is restrictive, with very little wiggle room. It is neither extremely expressive nor very musical. Because it is so comfortable and so safe, many if not most musicians limit themselves to this zone. **Comfort Zone = *mp* & *mf***

♪ The Safety Zone

Moving beyond the comfort zone into the safety zone offers dynamic possibilities that will make the music more beautiful, musical, and passionate. This zone is safe. This means you won't be breaking any rules or doing anything that might seem excessive or self-conscious. **Safety Zone = *p*, *mp*, *mf*, *f*.**

♪ The Extreme Zone

Moving beyond the safety zone into the extreme zone is a risk. It requires both focus and energy. You need to really pay attention, to really listen, and to explore and experiment. Performing in the extreme zone, you will make your music extremely beautiful, musical, and passionate. Knowing the extreme zone, its feel, its location, and its limits will ensure that you use the full range of dynamics offered by your instrument. **Extreme Zone = *pp*, *p*, *mp*, *mf*, *f*, *ff*.**

♪ The Outrageous Zone

Moving into the outrageous zone takes courage, intense energy, and intense focus. I believe that artists should be courageous. It is part of our job description. The outrageous zone must be explored, never forgotten, always touched upon. Using the outrageous zone, with some intuitive differentiation, will allow the music to be outrageously beautiful, musical, and passionate.

Becoming familiar with the outrageous zone will show you that it IS appropriate and that you can use it any time the feeling arises. Going overboard with "extremely delicate" is not such a danger. On the other hand, it is easy to go overboard with an extreme version of "forceful," something that creates true distortion and discomfort in the ears of the listener or with your fellow musicians. **Outrageous Zone = *ppp*, *pp*, *p*, *mp*, *mf*, *f*, *ff*, *fff*.**

♪ Not for Comfort and Safety

Music is not for our comfort and safety. Music is for our deeper tranquility, our passion, our excitement, our expression, our sanity, our health, our beauty, our love, our peace of mind, and our clarity. Get ready for the wonderful turbulence that performing music offers. Unfasten those seat belts and let your music soar!

Zones of Physical Intensity
And How They Might Feel

fff = Very Forceful — **Outrageous Zone**

ff = Forceful — **Extreme Zone**

f = Strong — **Safety Zone**

mf = Mildly Strong — **Comfort Zone**

Not much wiggle room if confined to this zone

mp = Mildly Delicate

p = Delicate — **Safety Zone**

pp = Very Delicate — **Extreme Zone**

ppp = Extremely Delicate — **Outrageous Zone**

INTENSITY

EXPRESSIVE RANGE

STILLNESS: Let's not take silence for granted. All dynamic levels arise from silence and stillness. This is where the real power in music comes from. Don't start from "extremely soft" or "extremely delicate." Start with the stillness which creates silence. There is a world of difference between *ppp* and Silence. Explore it and allow it to support you.

NOTE: The Outrageous Zone encompasses all the other zones, The Extreme Zone includes the Safety and Comfort Zones, and the Safety Zone includes the Comfort Zone.

♪ Exercises for Physical Intensity

The spectrum of performance possibilities ranges from physically uninhibited, to extremely delicate, to simply disappearing. If you are a "screamer," then "forceful" comes naturally and "delicate" may not be a natural part of your palette. In this case you must pay special attention to the extreme regions of delicate. If you are a very sweet, gentle, and delicate player, you need to understand how the energy behind "the scream" can actually get you exactly where you want to go. You should be conscious at all times of both extremes. Visualize them, and make them an integral part of your physical vocabulary.

The following exercises will help put the extreme ranges inside your head, into your muscles, into your touch, and inside every pore of your body.

Forceful

Playing "forcefully" means to play in a way that is physically uninhibited. The term "forceful" denotes "a very physical and muscular effort" that coincidentally results in "loud." In this experiment, "physicality" is the desired outcome and "loud" is secondary.

To take full advantage of this, we need only touch upon it at very special moments. For instance, I most often use a light touch (pressure) at the blues piano and frequently infuse my performance with momentary peaks of forcefulness. These "peaks" are not abrupt jumps, but smooth and sometimes fast crescendos followed by decrescendos. A sweet, sensitive passage can sound even sweeter through the subtle use of forceful moments. We must arm ourselves with this tool and understand how it can work for us.

Don't concern yourself with the tone or the sound of your instrument when practicing forcefulness. In the end, your sound will be better than ever. This exercise is about physical feeling, not tone. In most cases, the way to gauge if you are truly exploring the outer reaches of forceful is when your tone sounds bad because you are stressing the instrument. If you understand and experience what is "outside the box," you will know that you are fully using what is "inside the box." Then you can use the extremes with knowledge and musicality.

Warm Up for Forceful!

Before trying this exercise, make sure you warm up. This is especially important because you will be using as much physical force as possible for a short time. If you are not sufficiently warmed up, you could end up hurting yourself.

Note that different instruments and arrangements offer completely different circumstances. For instance, chords on the piano are easier to perform forcefully because you can use your arm muscles and put your whole body weight behind it. Finger movements are more difficult and can more easily leave you susceptible to injury. And of course, vocal chords can be damaged. For amplified instruments, set the amplification at a level where the loudest sound is no louder than an acoustic singing voice.

A List of Special Instructions for Approaching Forceful

1. Warm up.

2. Don't hurt yourself or damage your instrument.

3. Make sure you play the tune in the same tempo and same key for this exercise and the following exercises.

4. Play the beginning of the tune with INTENSE PHYSICALITY.

5. Play forcefully only long enough to establish the feeling of forcefulness in your body and mind. This shouldn't take more than a few seconds.

6. If this sounds only like a loud version of the way you normally play, apply even more physicality.

Next we'll take the same intensity we put into forceful and invite every pore to take part in the most intriguing exploration of all—the exploration of delicate.

Delicate

Welcome to the delicate zone. This is where it all happens. This is where you discover the true power in your music. There is a world of artistic intensity between "delicate" and *niente* (nothing) and between *pianissimo* (very quiet) and silence. In the delicate zone, we allow the immense powers of silence, intimacy, and subtlety to pervade our music. There are many obstacles at the entrance to the world of the delicate zone, so be brave.

As we have seen, one of the most powerful aspects in music is silence. Think about the effect of the space between words in the example in the section about Thor's Story (see page 18). Do you remember how the spaces placed within a sentence seem to support the message with amazing effectiveness? Think about that special feeling you experience while sitting in silence either in anticipation at the beginning of a performance or in reflection immediately following a finale. The power of rhythm and articulation is supported and defined by the silence between the sounds. Sound itself is a mix of the fluctuation of on-and-off, motion and stillness. Notice how you can experience the power of silence to varying degrees and at different dynamic levels, even when the music is filling the space. And remember, the essence of music is the play between sound and silence.

We tend to think of pianissimo as quieter than piano. But maybe we should think about pianissimo as a tiny bit more than stillness, which creates silence. This way, we honor silence and allow it to bring its extraordinary power into our music. Silence empowers music.

The territory between quiet and silence is derived from the physical experience of "extremely delicate" input. You can gauge your exploration of "extremely delicate" by the fact that some notes you sing or play do not actually come out. If all your notes come out and sound beautiful, you are probably not digging deep enough. If all your tones still sound pure to you, or if you feel like you are in control, you are probably not trying hard enough.

"Extremely delicate" is never harmful, so there is no need to hold back. You cannot hurt yourself or your instrument in the realm of "delicate." By making a practice of spending time on this feeling of extreme delicacy, you gain much more control over your music.

The initial part of this exercise does not require you to change your technique. Don't tilt the bow on the violin so fewer hairs are running across the strings. If you use a pick on the guitar, don't put it down because you think you can play more quietly with your fingers. Don't simply turn down your volume control. And if you are singing, don't close your lips to muffle the sound or whisper. Don't use a mute on a string or brass instrument. Using these techniques in performance is quite effective, but they do not help us accomplish our goal of instilling a more delicate feel into your physical system— and that is what you want to accomplish in these exercises.

Adjusting your own physical intensity, independent of the instrument, gives you a more direct experience of the intensity variation we are after. Remember, when we talk about dynamic variation, we create it through intensity variation. The "extremely delicate" zone takes as much focus and energy —perhaps even more focus and energy—as the "forceful" zone.

A List of Special Instructions for Approaching Delicate

1. Make sure you play the piece with the same tempo and in the same key as in the forceful part of the exercise.

2. When you play your song, focus on the physical. Don't worry about the sound. When notes begin to NOT come out, or when they sound ugly, you are finding the delicate extreme. This is good. Keep playing delicately. Eventually the notes will start coming out and the sound will improve.

3. For singers and wind players, it is important to keep the flow of air "supported." If the air stops, you may have reached beyond your normal ability to play delicately—this is good. Try to sing or play with the same delicacy, but support the air so it does not stop. Then try to take it to an even more delicate level.

4. Do not lose the rhythm. Support the rhythm with some intensity or physicality. This should not prevent or limit the extremes of delicacy.

5. Drummers who have trouble keeping the rhythm when playing delicately should notice how they move when playing forcefully: with heads bobbing, shoulders bopping, or bodies rocking. Try moving the same way, and with the same energy, but touch your sticks or hands to your instruments very delicately. Your focus and the energy should not decrease when playing delicately.

6. Absolute Rule: There are times when full tilt "forceful" is not appropriate. There is never a reason to exclude extreme delicate from your palette.

Extreme Dynamics and the Wiggles

There is an infinite number of ways to apply dynamics within the range of extremes. Even the least experienced of you can play the artist and express yourselves fully. When you apply block dynamics as well as dynamic flow, it comes out as wiggles. Wiggles can be applied subtly or intensely through the spontaneous and continuous flow of musical expression.

For instance, *mf* (mild) can be wiggled subtly to cover two dynamic increments such as *mp* to *mf* (mild to full), or *mf* to *f* (full to strong). It can be wiggled more intensely to cover three or more increments as mentioned previously. Although you may not use this extreme effect often, it is still good to have it in you repertoire. You may be surprised at how practical, useful, and musical this effect is when you use it in particular ways.

After playing and recording your songs or exercises in various ways and using different extremes, ask yourself (and others) a few questions from the famous lists of THE IMPORTANT QUESTIONS and THE ESSENTIAL QUESTIONS on pages 46 and 57. Which approach is the one with more dynamics or less dynamics? Which is more musical, more emotional, more exciting, more fun, has a richer tonal quality, is more alive, etc.?

Also ask yourself, "Is there absolutely too much dynamic variation in the music?" If the answer is "no," you should consider exploring even greater extremes of both intensity and frequency. If the answer is "yes," then mellow out the top part of your range and make sure the wiggles are smooth.

In theory, a performance can be too extreme, too abrupt, or too raucous on the upper end of the dynamic range. However, in my experience it is rare that someone really must mellow the upper range. By continuing to explore the extremes and having them at your fingertips for the appropriate moments, you will be able to tap fully into your individuality and self-expression.

Large Jumps

Big and immediate jumps UP from lower to upper dynamic ranges can be good for special effects and rhythmic feel. If your intention is flowing musicality, an abrupt jump up dynamically will distract from the melodic flow. The solution is to allow for a smoother connection from the delicate dynamic level to the more forceful dynamic level by applying a crescendo.

Big jumps DOWN from the higher dynamic levels to the lower dynamic levels are almost always very cool.

Even the least experienced of you can play the artist and express yourselves fully.

Part Three
Playing and Exploring

♪ Details for the One-Minute Exercise

Choose a piece of music you are very comfortable with—one you can repeat in exactly the same way every time you play it. If you choose a long piece, select a section from that piece.

♪ Establishing Dynamic Range

Both "delicate" and "forceful" uncover the elements necessary to produce rich sound and character in your performance. While you explore, don't worry if the instrument squeaks, chokes, flutters, distorts, sounds a little out of tune, or sounds scratchy in unacceptable ways. These things correct themselves very naturally, very quickly, and in the right way. Warm up first. Then play the section once before beginning the exercise.

Establish Forceful

To establish forceful, use your muscles and go over the top with uninhibited physicality. Don't hurt yourself or your instrument. Once you are absolutely sure you are over the top, you can stop.

Establish Delicate

As you play more delicately, the sound may stop coming out. This is good. If this happens, make the sound again, and then get even more delicate. Extreme delicate is a very important and effective dynamic for all performance. Don't give up too early. When you think you've got it, keep it going for a little more to ensure that you are established in the "delicate" zone.

Even though you can do this exercise in one minute, it is very important to put a lot of time into exploring and establishing your "delicate" zone. This helps your touch, your tone, your control, your technique, and the way you understand musical performance.

Wiggles

Let the dynamics flow **like the waves and ripples on the ocean.** Make sure you are touching upon the very delicate and forceful levels adequately. You can fluctuate the dynamics quickly by using micro-dynamics. Try to keep everything moving.

Tracks 14 through 19: Saxophone

In Tracks 14 through 19, Jim Gailloreto demonstrates how to establish a range and explore the wiggles. What you hear is an unrehearsed documentation of the results of this exploration.

Track 14: Saxophone—No Dynamics

Track 15: Saxophone—Forceful

Track 16: Saxophone—Extremely Delicate

Notice how Jim starts out "delicate" and then explores "extremely delicate."

Track 17: Saxophone—Wiggles Experiment A

Track 18: Saxophone—Wiggles Experiment B

Track 19: Saxophone—Wiggles Experiment C

Notice how each of these three wiggle experiments, Tracks 17, 18, and 19, are quite different from one another. You can hear the spontaneity in these performances. You may also notice some space available for more "forceful" playing.

NOTE: The fact is, though I prefer using extreme dynamics in my playing, they are part of a stylistic choice. Whether or not you choose to play with extreme dynamics, you should know them. If they are in your mind, in your soul, in your muscles and in every pore of your body, you will be able to call upon them when your heart is ready.

Record

Record everything—even the warm up—if you really want to hear what you are doing and open up your musical thinking and understanding. Go back and listen to the recording a day after you've made it. Compare the less dynamic performances with the more dynamic performances. Then compare smaller sections for each of the different performances. Notice the good qualities even if the dynamics seem too extreme at first. Then adjust your performance and record it again, comparing it with your first recording. During this process, ask yourself THE IMPORTANT QUESTIONS on page 46.

The value of this short exercise is that you can apply it to every aspect of a practice session as a way to keep the expressive range clearly established and at your fingertips. Why not make even scale exercises an expressive musical experience?

Here We Go

We have come now to the whole point of this book. This is the part that is easy to grasp. Everything up to this point was written mostly to break down barriers that suppress expression. Now you can just dig in and let your music soar!

A Note to Teachers, Directors, and Band Leaders

Because they rarely have much time, dynamic variation is usually the last thing teachers, directors, band leaders, and musicians work on, if they work on it at all. We have solved that problem for you! The following powerful exercise takes only ONE MINUTE!

The Incredible One-Minute Exercise

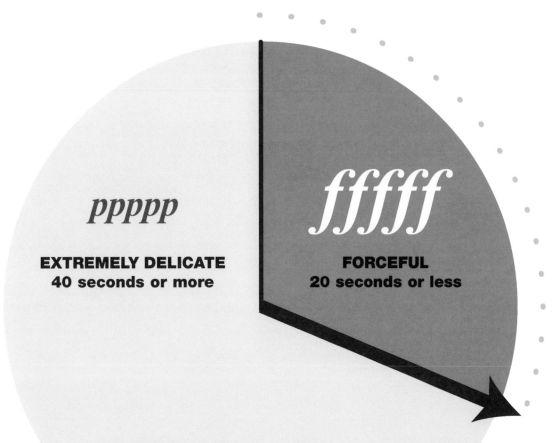

ppppp

EXTREMELY DELICATE
40 seconds or more

fffff

FORCEFUL
20 seconds or less

This exercise freshly imprints two extremes of an expressive range into your muscles, heart and mind, and opens up a broad palette for spontaneous, emotional and uninhibited self-expression. It works well for ensembles and individuals.

Choose a piece of music. After warming up, play the piece of music from the beginning with extreme forcefulness. Do this for only 20 seconds (or less, if you clearly have reached this extreme). Begin again, and with the rest of the time (at least 40 seconds), play the piece with extreme delicacy. Try and get deeper and deeper into delicacy and stillness as you go. That's "The Incredible One-Minute Exercise."

Now play the piece, making use of your full dynamic and expressive range. Touching upon both "forceful" and the stillness of "extreme delicate," constantly vary the intensity like the waves on the ocean. Think of your performance as one given by a great expressive artist—which you are.

Part Four
FAQs and Additional Suggestions

♪ Dry Room

Question: I need to project more when I am in a dry or dead-sounding room, so I leave out the quieter range. Should I play louder in quiet-sounding rooms?

Answer: When room acoustics influence how you approach playing your instrument, it can result in distorted "information" and disappointing results.

One of the great disappointments in musical performance is a stage or room with a dry sound. The room seems to suck the energy out of the performance. The sound seems to stick close to the surface of the instrument. Musicians in this situation often try to compensate by playing louder, but the sound is projected out only a few more feet. If you have an amplifier, you can turn it up, but the sound still seems to stick close to the amplifier's speakers. When you try too hard to project, you linger in the upper part of your dynamic range, rather than touch upon it, and as a result compromise your tonal quality and technique. Ignoring your "delicate" zone shrinks your dynamic range even more than whatever the room is doing to it! And, you eliminate your connection to the power of silence. Limiting dynamics does not change the "deadness" of the experience.

This can all be avoided. Compromising tone and dynamic range won't make the music better. As you go from "echoey" shower to muffled den, from cave to dense forest, from canyon to soundproof room, there are things that remain the same. The limits of your instrument and your technique do not change. The answer is in your touch. Play the way you know how to play and let the sound do what it has to do. Understand the difference between dynamic variation and intensity variation. Focus only on your physical connection to the instrument. *Forte* feels strong and *pianissimo* feels delicate. Use motion and touch instead of the sound as a focus point.

Dry Room and Amplification

If you are amplified, adding a little reverb may not help your own sonic experience but it can improve the sound for the audience. This can be more problematic if it forces you to change your normal physical intensity level. It is better to "get some ears out there" to give you an honest assessment of the sound from different points in the room. Making the music sound good to you on stage may ruin the sound in the audience.

Monitors, in general, play havoc with the house sound. Keep the monitor levels down as much as possible, or off. Try using the monitors for vocals only!

♪ Live Room—Too Loud

Question: If the room is live, should I cut back on my louder dynamics?

Answer: In some situations, playing forcefully on an acoustic instrument, even for a moment, might be too loud for the room and the eardrums of the audience. In these rare cases, it's best to leave forceful playing out. Be very careful if you play brass or loud percussion. Never play so loud that it creates a physically unpleasant experience.

♪ Amplified Music: What Is Too Loud?

Amplified music is usually too loud. I define "too loud" as when the music is uncomfortable to either members of the audience or to other musicians on stage. If the music makes members of the audience uncomfortable, you are physically damaging ears, and you are limiting your career. You can turn down the amplifier and still get the extreme physical and wild effect you want, with even better results, as well as better sonic quality.

Janis Joplin once approached me during a show at the Avalon Ballroom in San Francisco. We were both very young, physical, and had wild blues bands. Janis wanted to know how my group, Siegel-Schwall, got such a strong audience reaction and yet didn't play loud. I answered, "Dynamics." In those days, the dynamics we used were very basic and primitive, yet they were highly effective for live musical performances.

Two rock bands that I coached experienced dramatic results. I didn't mention to them that loud music could destroy both their hearing and their audience's hearing. All I did was get them to turn their amplifiers way down and apply dynamics. Their faces lit up when they experienced all the power in their performance at a lower volume. They were so excited they were bursting. One group even said they would never play so loud again—at least not at the level where ear plugs might be a consideration. One group reported that the audience responded more and that the club owner began hiring them back more often.

Both groups asked me how they could make sure that they would not start turning their amplification up again, since that is a tendency for all musicians. I shared two ideas with them. First, I suggested something that Siegel-Schwall did many years ago: start quiet and then turn the amps on stage down even more on the second song. Second, I suggested that the group members control each other's volume.

In a concert setting, the best way to control amplification is to collaborate with all the members of the group and crew to set a very low stage volume, one that is set at a level that the sound engineer can work with. Set the volume and leave it alone unless the sound engineer requests that members on stage make adjustments. Keep the use of monitors to a minimum (try just a small touch of vocals in the monitors and then only a slight amount of anything else if absolutely necessary). This approach takes getting used to, but it is worth the effort.

Most of us musicians, even classical players, have the tendency to try to project more than is necessary during a performance. When we are armed with amplifiers, the result can be exaggerated, sometimes to the point of sounding too loud.

♪ Control

Question: Can I lose control if I dive into playing with the dynamics?

Answer: If you are talking about technical control over the instrument the answer is no, although there are usually some short-term challenges. It just takes a little getting used to. Wanting to maintain control over the results can be the bigger problem! We need to let go of some control so the muse and our hearts can get involved and have some fun once in a while. Spontaneity is an essential ingredient in the expressive process and sometimes the desire to control the outcome can get in the way. Go for it!

♪ Not Ready For Dynamics

Question: My student is only four years old and has been playing for only six months. Is this too early to apply dynamics?

Answer: Beginning players might want to have at least one piece under their fingers first, but applying dynamics early in the learning curve—if the student likes it—may actually quicken the learning process. I have coached young children into dynamic phrasing in a very short period of time, and it really helped their playing and their confidence. I recommend practicing with dynamics during all phases of the learning process, whether you are just learning your instrument, or whether you are starting on a new piece of music. It will help ensure that you remember to play with dynamics during a performance!

♪ Clarification: Playing Within Your Capabilities

If the desire is to be fully expressive and present a beautiful performance—whether it is just for yourself or for an audience—I suggest you choose works that are well within your capabilities. You should be able to "nail" all the aspects of the work like the pitch and rhythm. If the works are somewhat challenging, it might feel like you are constantly on the verge of stumbling. That could be very distracting to both you and the listener if that's all you are offering. So consider the degree of challenge you want to take on for these occasions, and perhaps challenge yourself more at other times.

♪ More Audio Examples

Track 20: Rhythm Bass—Some Dynamics

Track 21: Rhythm Bass—Wiggles

Bob Lizik, who is Brian Wilson's (The Beach Boys) bass player, stopped by my studio to visit with me. I described what I was recording and had him try this experiment. Track 20 and Track 21 are examples of Bob's spontaneous and unrehearsed application of an extreme range of dynamic flow.

You can also listen to audio examples on the Web: www.chamberblues.com/soar

Track 22: Violin Solo

Track 22 is by Rachel Barton-Pine, an artist whose natural artistic sensitivity includes the constant flow of extreme dynamics. The work is a composition of mine called *Opus 11*, from the *Chamber Blues Suite*. The first page of the musical score is included here. You can find the full score online at www.chamberblues.com/soar.

> *For those of you who don't read music, please don't feel intimidated by the score. Music notation is not music. It is a mathematical language that represents sonic happenings, and it provides a way of communicating musical ideas and recording them. There are musicians of all kinds, including great and renowned virtuosi, who don't read music. However, if you are interested in learning the language of music notation, it is quite simple and it can be helpful in many ways.*

Opus 11 for Solo Violin

From the Chamber Blues Suite by Corky Siegel © 1990

Biographical Notes

Corky Siegel has earned an international reputation as a master of the blues harmonica. He is also a pianist, singer-songwriter, and national award-winning composer.

In 1965, Corky teamed up with guitarist Jim Schwall and landed a steady engagement as the house band at the world-renowned Pepper's Show Lounge in Chicago. Corky performed there weekly with historic blues icons Muddy Waters, Howlin' Wolf, Willie Dixon, Little Walter, and others. This experience, and a record deal on Vanguard Records, launched the Siegel-Schwall Band career.

Shortly after that, Corky met a music titan who would change his life. Maestro Seiji Ozawa introduced Corky as guest soloist to many of the world's top-tier orchestras, bringing blues and classical music together. Live performances with orchestras such as the New York Philharmonic and the Chicago and Boston Symphonies received critical acclaim, while their recordings received global recognition such as the French Grand Prix du Disque.

Corky's collaborations with symphony orchestras led him to receive four separate commissions to compose Symphonic Blues works. In 1987, he founded the ground-breaking group Chamber Blues. He continues to tour world-wide with major symphonies and with his groups, Siegel-Schwall and Chamber Blues.

Corky has recorded numerous projects on RCA/Wooden Nickel, Vanguard, Gadfly, Deutsche Grammophon, and Alligator Records. You can go to chamberblues.com for detailed biographical information, recordings, and more. Corky's recordings are also available at other web sites and record stores.

Peter Krammer is an entrepreneur, guitarist, and composer living in northern California. He has scored sound tracks for dance theater and independent films. He performs regularly with jazz groups in the San Francisco Bay Area.

Credits and Gratitude from Corky

Illustrations: By Holly Tucker Siegel. That's my dear wife, best friend, and my partner in every breath.

Yoga: I have been a student of Yoga since 1974. The inward contemplation that brought me these revelations about music was guided by my beloved Gurus, Swami Muktananda and Swami Chidvilasananda. My intent is to reflect their beautiful teaching, but I can't be sure to what degree my writing has succeeded in that sense. Either way, I owe this book and my joyful life to my Gurus and to my sister, Joy, who introduced me to them.

About seven years ago, right out of nowhere and to my great surprise and pleasure, Swami Chidvilasananda began speaking emphatically and eloquently about dynamic variation as a way to enhance the practice of chanting. This event took place in a special music course I attended at the Ashram in South Fallsburg, New York. Because I've been conducting workshops on dynamic variation constantly since 1973, because I named myself "the fanatic" on this subject, and because I've been trying to write a book on the subject, this was an amazing synchronicity for me. I never heard anyone speak about dynamics in this way. Not the teachers, and not the musicians. My own Guru spoke about that most obscure and secret subject of dynamic variation, the thing that happened to be my own odd compulsion! I felt directed by the universe to make it a profound responsibility to complete this book.

Peter Krammer: I felt I couldn't do this alone. I had twenty years of writing, but with my life as a composer, touring with Siegel-Schwall, Chamber Blues, symphony orchestras, solo performances, and the music business/self-management responsibilities I share with Holly, finishing this book seemed unrealistic.

A student of mine became a very close friend. A brilliant fellow. As a true lover of nature and the arts, he really understood the importance of sharing this topic with the world. He agreed to help me. That's Pete. When I want to dig deeply into a concept with others, most people will just leave the room. Pete has always been willing to dig deeply into the esoteric in search of practical answers and solutions. I needed someone who really understood and wasn't going to be satisfied by just scratching the surface. Together we have completed this book. It only took us seven years. (Pete's wife, Annette, designed the layout of the book.)

Jim Kanas (guitarist and educator): Jim told me that he never used the word "loud" when teaching children because they might mistake "loud" for "rowdy." This started me thinking about describing the whole dynamic range in terms that related directly to the emotional and physical aspects of playing. This simple statement provided me with many valuable ideas and applications. Thank you, Jim.

Tom Dundee: When I began offering workshops, specifically about the music business, I spoke about how even the most special and loved artists can be overlooked by the music industry. My dear friend, Tom Dundee, was one of my two best examples. (James Lee Stanley was the other.) I never talked about the music industry without telling a story about Tom. People and audiences loved to be around Tom; he exuded so much joy and he was absolutely irresistible—on- or off-stage. All of us, colleagues who knew Tom, and I—considered him one of the best singer-songwriters and performers around. When I was playing with the Siegel-Schwall Band and thinking of going "solo" in 1974, it was Tom's example of how a simple, down to earth, and even laid-back offering by one guy singing and playing can be filled with intense power and magic. At his live concerts, Tom used dynamics in an extreme way, and always came off cool and collected. Tom was one of my greatest influences in this way, and while I wrote this book he came to mind constantly.

We dedicate this book to Tom Dundee. As I write these very last words of this twenty-three-year project, I contemplate what I have gained by knowing Tom. He died in April 2006, just a few days before we finished this book, from a motorcycle accident that happened two blocks from my house.

Corky Siegel